Books in Spanish
for Children and Young Adults:
An Annotated Guide

Libros Infantiles y Juveniles
en Español:
Una Guía Anotada

by

ISABEL SCHON

The Scarecrow Press, Inc.
Metuchen, N.J. & London
1978

Library of Congress Cataloging in Publication Data

Schon, Isabel.
    Books in Spanish for children and young adults.

    English and Spanish.
    Includes indexes.
    1.   Children's literature, Spanish--Bibliography.
2.   Children's literature, Spanish American--Bibliography.
I.   Title.   II.   Title: Libros infantiles y juveniles en
español.
Z2694. 5. S35   [PN1009. S8]   028. 52   78-10299
ISBN 0-8108-1176-6

To my husband,
Dr. Richard R. Chalquest

to my daughter,
Verita

and to all the young readers
who inspired me

PREFACE

This book is intended to serve as a guide to any adult --teacher, librarian, counselor, layman or parent--who is interested in selecting books in Spanish written by Hispanic authors for children of preschool through high school age. Most of the books included in this guide were published after 1973, and come from Argentina, Chile, Colombia, Costa Rica, Cuba, Ecuador, Guatemala, Mexico, Peru, Puerto Rico, Spain, Uruguay and Venezuela.

I have identified books for children and young adults that highlight the lifestyle, folklore, heroes, history, fiction, poetry, theatre, and classical literature of Hispanic cultures as expressed by Hispanic authors. Therefore, no translations or textbooks are included. Though such an undertaking is overly ambitious, I have attempted to include most books that are readily available in Spanish-speaking countries and that represent the books that Hispanic young readers are now reading in their own countries. None of the books reviewed was out-of-print as of January 1978. To assist the selector, I have used the following symbols with each book annotated:

*   Asterisks denote outstanding book: entertaining reading with a high potential for reader involvement or interest.

m   Marginal book: may be used to supplement a collection; but the book may be difficult to read, may lack attractive illustrations, or may lack reader appeal.

nr   Not Recommended: mostly dull books.

I have also indicated a tentative grade level for each book, but the individual student's Spanish reading ability, interest, taste, and purpose should be the main criteria for determining the true level of each book.

The selector will also note that a few Spanish-speaking countries are not represented in this book and that Spain and Argentina have the greatest number of books for young readers. This reflects the actual state of the publishing industry for young readers in Spanish-speaking countries. Books are still an expensive luxury in many Spanish-speaking countries.

To assist selectors in ordering these books, I have included in Appendix I the names and addresses of dealers in Spanish-speaking countries that in my experience will expedite shipment of any order. These dealers are highly recommended for their efficiency and prompt service. I have also included in Appendix II a list of book dealers in the United States that specialize in books from Spanish-speaking countries. Unfortunately, not all of the books recommended in this guide are now available in the United States.

It is my sincere hope that this book will assist all readers in understanding the heritage of Hispanic people as well as appreciating the beauty and variety of Hispanic customs through the writings of Hispanic authors.

I wish to express my appreciation to my husband, Dr. R. R. Chalquest, for his patience and encouragement; to the many librarians in the Spanish-speaking countries for their gracious cooperation; to the Faculty Research Grant Committee, College of Education, Arizona State University for its support; to the professional staff of the University Library, Arizona State University, for their marvelous assistance; and to Ms. Susan Garvin for her collaboration.

Isabel Schon, Ph.D.
Assistant Professor in Library Science
Arizona State University, Tempe
January 1978

PROLOGO

La intención de este libro es la de servir como guía
a cualquier adulto, ya sea profesor, bibliotecario, consejero,
o padre, que esté interesado en seleccionar libros en español
escritos por autores hispanos para jóvenes de edad preescolar
hasta la secundaria. La mayoría de los libros incluídos en
este guía han sido publicados después de 1973 en Argentina,
Chile, Colombia, Costa Rica, Cuba, Ecuador, Guatemala,
México, Perú, Puerto Rico, España, Uruguay y Venezuela.

He identificado libros infantiles y juveniles que
demuestran el estilo de vida, folklore, héroes, historia,
ficción, poesía, teatro, y literatura clásica de las culturas
hispanas como han sido expresadas por autores hispanos.
Por lo tanto, no he incluido traducciones ni libros de texto.
Aun cuando mi empresa es demasiado ambiciosa, he tratado
de incluir el mayor número, de los libros que están
disponibles en países hispanos y los libros que leen ahora
los jóvenes lectores hispanos en sus propios países. Ninguno
de los libros reseñados estaban agotado hasta enero de 1978.
Para ayudar al selector, he usado los siguientes símbolos
con cada libro anotado:

* Asteriscos significan libro sobresaliente: lectura
    divertida con un gran potencial de interesar al
    lector.

m Libro Mediocre: puede ser usado para completar una
    colección, pero el libro puede ser difícil de leer,
    y ser deficiente en ilustraciones o deficiente en
    atractivos para el lector.

nr No Recomendables: casi siempre libros aburridos.

También he indicado un grado tentativo de lectura para cada
libro, pero el nivel de lectura de cada lector, así como sus
intereses, gustos y propósitos, deben ser los criterios más
importantes para determinar el nível verdadero de cada libro.

vii

El selector también notará que algunos países hispanos no están representados en este libro y que España y Argentina tienen el mayor número de libros para jóvenes lectores. Esto refleja el estado actual de la industria editorial para jóvenes en países hispanos. En muchos países hispanos libros son todavía un lujo muy caro.

Para ayudar a los selectores en ordenar estos libros, he incluido en el Apéndice I los nombres y direcciónes de negociantes en países hispanos que en mi experiencia apresurarán el envío de cualquier orden. Estos negociantes son eficientes y procuran dar un buen servicio. También he incluido en el Apéndice II una lista de negociantes de libros en los Estados Unidos que se especializan en libros de países hispanos. Desgraciadamente, no todos los libros recomendados en este guía están disponibles ahora en los Estados Unidos.

Mis más sinceros deseos son que este libro ayude a todos los lectores a comprender la herencia cultural, la belleza y la variedad de costumbres hispanas como han sido expresadas por autores hispanos.

Quisiera expresar mi agradecimiento a mi esposo, Dr. R. R. Chalquest, por su paciencia y apoyo, a las bibliotecarias de todos los países hispanos por su amable ayuda al Comité de Investigaciones de la Facultad de Pedagogía de Arizona State University por su apoyo, al personal de la biblioteca de Arizona State University por su valiosa ayuda, y a la Srta. Susan Garvin por su colaboración.

Dra. Isabel Schon
Profesora en Biblioteconomia
Arizona State University, Tempe
enero 1978

TABLE OF CONTENTS

ARGENTINA

FICTION

m   Alegría, Fernando. <u>La ciudad de arena.</u> Illus: Juan Marchesi. (Buenos Aires: Ediciones de la Flor, 1974. 28p.) Gr. 1-3.

    Busy, colorful illustrations and long, intricate text tell the story of a sand city. Four children build a beautiful city with castles, townsquares, and even a sea aquarium for entertainment. At the end of the day a big wave pulls in the entire city, and the children play again by the sea.

nr Bird, Poldy. <u>El país de la infancia.</u> (Buenos Aires: Ediciones Orión, 1977. 160p.) Gr. 10-adult.

    Even though the author believes that this collection of her "stories" (essays) will be enjoyed by children ages eight to thirteen, I cannot imagine young readers being interested in the author's feelings and thoughts about the joys of motherhood, the responsibilities of personal liberty, the fears of aging, etc. Perhaps some parents will enjoy sharing another adult's thoughts about life, religion, and parenthood, but this is definitely not a book for young readers.

nr Bornemann, Elsa Isabel. <u>Cuadernos de un delfín.</u> Illus: Alberto Peri. (Buenos Aires: Editorial Plus Ultra, 1976. 94p.) Gr. 7-10.

    Unbelievable love-story between an adolescent dolphin and its trainer, a young woman. Long descriptions of the dolphin's feelings and man's mistreatment of marine life, as well as an affected emphasis on "good" values make this a tedious story about marine life.

nr Calny, Eugenia. <u>Conejita blanca y el viaje a la luna.</u>

1

Illus: Chacha. (Buenos Aires: Editorial Plus Ultra, 1976. 45p.) Gr. 3-6.

Collection of ten moralistic stories that pretend to teach children to be useful in life, to appreciate the beauty of life, to cherish their loved ones, etc. The attractive animal illustrations should be the only aspect of this pretentious book that might be shown to children, otherwise young readers will find reading a tedious exercise in morality.

nr Cané, Cora. El buzo loco y otras aventuras. Illus: Viviana Barletta. (Buenos Aires: Editorial Plus Ultra, 1976. 95p.) Gr. 4-7.

The editors pretend to make reading a creative endeavor by selecting "aesthetic stories with up-to-date criteria." This vague statement reflects the uninspired and monotonous eight stories that have been "carefully selected." Some of the stories have a subtle moralistic intent, others a strong educational tone, but they are all wearisome to read.

* Cané, Miguel. Juvenilia. Illus: Santos Martínez Koch. (Buenos Aires: Editorial Kapelusz, 1965. 159p.) Gr. 9-12.

The schooldays of a teenager in Buenos Aires during the latter part of the 1800's are entertainly described with witty illustrations. The deserved punishments, close friends, cherished teachers, outside diversions and interesting classes are told through the eyes of the author who sometimes fondly and sometimes sadly remembers his adolescent years in a boys' school. The simple text and unaffected language will appeal to teenagers.

nr Cartosio, Emma de. Cuentos del perdido camino. Illus: Luis Pollini. (Buenos Aires: Editorial Plus Ultra, 1976. 93p.) Gr. 4-8.

Tedious collection of eight complicated stories that stress God's goodness, the power of love to forgive, giving happiness to your fellow men, patience and faith, and understanding among nations. Hopefully this dull, conceited book will not stifle any child's interest in reading.

m Cupit, Aaron. Amigo Chum. Illus: Chacha. (Buenos

Aires: Editiones Plus Ultra, 1975. 46p.) Gr. 3-6.

The editor's concern in contributing "valuable children's literature" have watered-down this collection of eleven dog adventure stories. Chum, an enthusiastic little dog, is seen in his various adventures after his escape: at the circus, on the farm, in the amusement park, on television, at the supermarket, on a ship, etc. Unfortunately long detailed descriptions and pretentious admonitions detract from the enjoyment of Chum's adventures.

nr _____. Cuentos para chicos de hoy en el mundo de ayer. (Buenos Aires: Conjunta Editores, 1977. 79p.) Gr. 6-8.

Pretentious collection of eight stories that attempt to reflect today's reality, but that will certainly bore young readers with its incessant moralizing and continuous teachings. Long descriptions and endless narrations result in complicated, uninteresting stories about clocks, spring, television, tape recorders, and others.

* _____. El país de los ojos transparentes. Illus: Santos Martínez Koch. (Buenos Aires: Editorial Sigmar, 1976. 20p.) Gr. 3-6.

Benjamin experiences fantastic adventures with a man and a beautiful girl who arrived from outer space. Attractive, colorful illustrations complement Benjamin's strange happenings with his new friends, such as encountering a magic table that serves delicious foods and an enchanting street that offers the most beautiful clothes.

m Estrada, Silvina. Un día en la vida de Juan Trébol. Illus: Alicia Charré. (Buenos Aires: Ángel Estrada, 1975. 18p.) Gr. 2-4.

Poetic description of a pasture that recalls the old times. Scenic illustrations of a lagoon, a windmill, forest animals and handsome colts that express their fears of a new, big, red machine. The complicated text and long, tedious descriptions of nature's feelings make this a slow-moving story.

m Finkel, Berta. Castillito de papel. Illus: Kitty Lorefice

de Passalia. (Buenos Aries: Editorial Plus Ultra, 1976. 46p.) Gr. 2-4.

This is a collection of eighteen stories and poems for children with attractive illustrations. Only the poems, such as "La hoja seca" (p. 15), "La foca" (p. 19), "Respuestas" (p. 11), and "El Escarabajo" (p. 39) are written in simple language; the stories are monotonous with a subtle moralistic undertone.

nr Franco, Luis. El zorro y su vecindario. Illus: Chacha. (Buenos Aires: Editorial Plus Ultra, 1976. 93p.) Gr. 7-9.

Pretentious vocabulary and interminable descriptions make this collection of animal stories a cheerless endeavor. The author pretended to write for teenagers about birds in flight, foxes and tigers in their natural surroundings, and the nobility of dogs, horses, and other animals. The results are twenty-eight uninspired stories with, however, surprisingly appealing, simple illustrations.

* Gallardo, Sara. Los dos amigos. Illus: Alicia Charré. (Buenos Aires: Editorial Estrada, 1974. 18p.) Gr. K-3.

Pleasing illustrations and simple text tell the adventures of a boy who found a fox in the forests of Argentina. They became good friends, and when the boy had to go to school, he decided to take the fox to school too. Problems with teachers during class time and special activities caused the fox to be asked to leave the classroom. The boy cried, but he was delightfully surprised when he was met by the fox on his way home. "School is not for him," thought the boy and they continued being the best friends in the world.

m Gambaro, Griselda. La cola mágica. Illus: Juan Marchesi. (Buenos Aires: Ediciones de la Flor, 1975. 28p.) Gr. 1-3.

Epaminondas, a funny dog, had a curious problem: he had the longest tail in the world. He had problems crossing the streets before the lights turned red, and he had problems walking in the forest without getting his tail tangled up in the trees. But it was a magic tail

for the children who sat on it and sailed through the sky.
Bold, colorful illustrations add interest to the sometimes
difficult text.

nr   Giménez Pastor, Marta.   En el cielo las estrellas.
     Illus: Luis Pollini.   (Buenos Aires: Editorial Plus
     Ultra, 1977.   47p.)   Gr. 3-6.

     Mediocre collection of twenty-three poems and
     stories that will confuse and/or bore young readers.
     Although the diverse themes are appealing to children,
     the long "educational" descriptions are unnecessary and
     needlessly complicated.   It includes dull stories about
     angels, clowns, trips, shoeshine boys, etc.

nr   _____.   La pancita del gato.   Illus: Kitty Lorefice
     de Passalia.   (Buenos Aires: Editorial Plus Ultra,
     1976.   45p.)   Gr. 1-3.

     Even though this collection of stories and poems
     won the 1975 Children's Literature Award from the soci-
     ety of Argentinean Writers, it offers very little for the
     pleasure of children.   The tedious, lifeless stories are
     impossible to enjoy and most of the poems are written
     in a most confusing and complicated style.   Also, un-
     fortunately, it has only a few illustrations.

m   Gomara, Susana López de.   Aires nuevos en Buenos
     Aires.   (Buenos Aires: Editorial Acme, 1976.   202p.)
     Gr. 9-adult.

     Long novel which describes life in Spanish Colonial
     times in Argentina.   Unfortunately the author tried to
     include too many aspects of the people and the political
     and military situation that make this novel long and con-
     fusing.   There is the life of the slaves in Argentinean
     homes, the English attack on Buenos Aires in 1806, the
     escape of the Spanish Viceroy, the patriotism of the
     people defending their country, the loves, joys and sor-
     rows of two families, the defeat of the English, and the
     lives and interests of the young.   The simple vocabulary
     and fast-moving story make this novel attractive to a
     sophisticated high-school reader.

nr   _____.   Las lunas de Juan Luna.   (Buenos Aires:
     Editorial Plus Ultra, 1975.   140p.)   Gr. 9-12.

This is the tedious story of Juan Luna, a boy from
Argentina, and his angel who protects him.   Even though
it is written in short chapters that supposedly describe
different adventures, the most pretentious and spiritless
style will not interest any adolescent.   The thoughts and
feelings of Juan Luna are lost among the obscure descriptions and lethargic happenings.

* Granata, María. El bichito de luz sin luz.   Illus: Raul
Stevano.   (Buenos Aires: Editorial Sigmar, 1976.   20p.)
Gr. 1-3.

A beetle embarks on a heart-warming search for his
lost light.   All his friends try to help him: a bird sug-
gests an electric battery, a pigeon tries carrying him,
a snake proposes lighting matches, a magpie gives him
a mirror, and finally the sun gives him a piece of sunlight that penetrates his body forever.   Handsome illustrations complement this delightful animal story.

* Grée, Alain. Yo quiero ser capitán.   (Buenos Aires:
Editorial Sigmar, 1973.   12p.) Gr. 3-6.

Through the eyes of a young captain, the reader is
introduced to different kinds of ships, such as caravels,
Viking, pirate, freight, passenger and fishing boats.   The
simple descriptions and attractive illustrations make
this an appealing story for young readers.

nr Lacau, María Hortensia. Yo y Honerín.   Illus: Mane
Bernardo.   (Buenos Aires: Editorial Plus Ultra, 1973.
76p.) Gr. 3-6.

Long tedious descriptions and textbook-like presentation make this a deadly book for children, though the illustrations are colorful.   The author bores the reader
with her endless religious and educational admonitions
and her affected sugar-coated writing style.   The twelve
chapters are the result of the author's childhood dreams,
games and inventions which may be of interest to her-
self, but, perhaps should have remained untold.

* Lamas, Norma. Los sueños del astronauta.   Illus:
Luis Pollini. (Buenos Aires: Conjunta Editores, 1975.
12p.) Gr. K-3.

Striking, colorful illustrations and no text; this book

may be used to invent stories about astronauts' dreams. The lack of text may detract from its appeal to older readers, but a simple story could be invented to tell to young readers.

* Ledesma, Roberto. Juan Sin Miedo. (Buenos Aires: Editorial Plus Ultra, 1975. 207p.) Gr. 9-12.

Adventure story set in Argentina that enthralls the reader by its candid characters, its fast-moving action and its varied scenery. Juan Sin Ruido, the humble hero, does not want to enlist in the white man's army, but he is anxious to help his fellow men. His services are certainly welcomed when the brave and charming Mercedes is kidnapped by the Indians. After many daring escapades fighting Indians, wild animals and inhospitable deserts and forests, Juan Sin Miedo returns Mercedes to her family. Mercedes, a strong and lovable young woman, does not forget her savior, and also performs a daring act to save her hero. At the end both decide to share a most difficult life together.

Some readers might object to the unkind description of the Indians and their "savage" acts (p. 152).

nr Lira Gaiero, Elsa. El solecito Andrés. Illus: Raul Fortin. (Buenos Aires: Editorial Plus Ultra, 1976. 46p.) Gr. 3-6.

Collection of five long, tedious stories about animals and the sun that are impossible to enjoy. The bold, two-tone illustrations are the only redeeming aspects of this book. Lifeless descriptions of the sun, a toad, a worm, and a cricket are artificially combined with uninspired adventures.

* Llega un hermanito. (Buenos Aires: Editorial Sigmar, n. d. 6p.) Gr. K-3.

Short, attractive story with pleasing illustrations of a little girl and her feelings upon the arrival of a baby brother. The simple vocabulary shows Mama pregnant, nursing baby, dressing the nude baby boy, and finally the little girl enjoys the undivided attention of Papa and Mama when baby sleeps.

* Mainar, Horacio L. El capitán Vermejo. (Buenos

Aires: Editorial Guadalupe, 1974. 126p.) Gr. 9-12.

    This is the adventurous life of a courageous officer
in nineteenth-century Argentina. It is a daring life that
represents an epoch and a social class of South America
that fought for independence. It describes colonial life
in Buenos Aires; the easy surrender of Buenos Aires to
the English in 1806; the mercy shown to the Inca, Huaina
Tupac, by the gallant officer; all told in a fast-moving
pace including fearless duels, heroic battles and valiant
actions.

m   Malinow, Inês. ¡Aquíii, Inosito! Illus: Alicia Portilla.
    (Buenos Aires: Editorial Plus Ultra, 1976. 45p.) Gr.
    3-6.

    Lively illustrations and fast-moving text (though long
and difficult) tell the adventures of Inosito, a charming
teddy bear. Inosito experiences fear before a vaccina-
tion, joy going to a picnic, doubts about a foreign visi-
tor, and many other feelings in his active life. Fewer
descriptions would make this book an adorable story for
young readers.

*   _____. Muchas veces cuatro patas. Illus: Nestor
    Luis Battagliero. (Buenos Aires: Editorial Sigmar,
    1976. 20p.) Gr. 1-3.

    A well-known veterinarian accepts Gaby as his as-
sistant when he visits sick animals. Gaby's common-
sense approach makes a sad dog happy, a kangaroo
start jumping again, and a cat start eating. Appealing
animal illustrations add interest to the sometimes long
text.

nr Marcuse, Aida E. Marcelo casi-casi.... (Buenos
    Aires: Editorial Paidos, 1976. 39p.) Gr. 3-6.

    The author wrote this diary to teach young readers
safety around the house and to avoid dangerous situations.
Children are cautioned against leaving toys on the floor,
pulling down tablecloths, playing with electric cords,
swallowing medicine pills, drinking cleaning solutions,
etc. This is definitely not children's recreational reading, but a naive sermon for parents.

nr Martí, José. La edad de oro. Illus: Lorenzo Amengual.

(Buenos Aires: Editorial Nueva Senda, 1972. 143p.)
Gr. 4-10.

This is a collection of the four copies of the magazine La Edad de Oro originally published in 1889 by José Martí in New York. It includes stories for children, history lessons and scientific facts that Martí considered to be valuable information for young readers of the nineteenth century. This edition contains striking, colorful illustrations, but the tedious, educational essays and stories will be of interest only to historians who are examining old children's books. Martí proposed to "contarles a las niñas cuentos lindos con que entretener a sus visitas y jugar con sus muñecas; y para decirles a los niños lo que deben saber para ser de veras hombres" (p. 6).

m Martín, Susana. Aventuras de dos muchachos que buscaban un papá. Illus: Alberto Peri. (Buenos Aires: Editorial Plus Ultra, 1977. 110p.) Gr. 7-12.

The sad adventures of two orphan brothers anxiously looking for a father are described in a fast-moving text. The great variety of adventures narrated, such as life in the orphanage, a long truck ride, an unhappy voyage on a whaling ship, etc. might interest young readers. Unfortunately, the sorrowful life of the two brothers and the author's message: "a father is the one who cares for us," adds an unnecessary moralistic tone to the story.

m Marval, Carlota. La casa de Madre Señora. (Buenos Aires: Editorial Plus Ultra, 1975. 100p.) Gr. 7-10.

The author has written a collection of twenty-three stories based on her own childhood memories in Buenos Aires. A few especially interesting stories are "Anacleta Godoy, para servir a Usted" (p. 17), which is a vivid, human description of the importance of a servant in the life of an Argentinean family, "Si me esperan voy y vuelvo" (p. 41), an amusing story of milkmen and their early activities, and "El Pavo Emancipado" (p. 81), which describes the family preparations of a Christmas turkey.

nr Mercader, Marta. Conejitos con hijitos. Illus: Jorge Pechersky. (Buenos Aires: Editorial Plus Ultra, 1977. 68p.) Gr. 3-6.

Monotonous collection of ten stories that narrate the "mischiefs and adventures" of little bunnies. Unending descriptions and complicated vocabulary result in wearisome reading in which even the little bunnies' adventures are difficult to find.

m   Morilla de Campbell, Julia. Adiós, Canopus. (Buenos Aires: Editorial Plus Ultra, 1976. 158p.) Gr. 9-12.

Through the eyes of a twelve-year-old girl, the reader is exposed to life in an Argentinean farm in the 1940's, as well as participating in an adventurous journey in a house on wheels called Canopus. The trip is planned by Julia's grandparents for the purpose of living for a few months in the interior of the Misiones jungle in northeast Argentina. Long descriptions and unnecessary educational accounts detract from the enjoyment of this adventure story.

nr   _____. Crines al viento. (Buenos Aires: Editorial Plus Ultra, 1977. 156p.) Gr. 9-12.

This is the tedious story of Manantial, "a white, brave and wise horse," that wanted to learn all about Argentina, and, therefore, "appreciate Argentina's many values." So, in the company of Nicolás, a twelve-year-old orphan, they embark on an educational journey throughout Argentina. The educational intent and the virtue of loving animals result in a dull and uninspired geographical description of Argentina.

nr   _____. El rey aventuras de un condor neuquino. (Buenos Aires: Plus Ultra, 1977. 150p.) Gr. 6-8.

Through the life of a couple of condors, the author aims to teach young people "the feelings and customs of condors as well as to demonstrate the individuality of Neuquén" (an area in northern Argentina). Tedious descriptions of the animals' feelings and thoughts about love, life, marriage, children, etc. make this story unappealing to animal lovers. And, even though the author intended to reveal to young readers the fascinating magic of Argentina, I am afraid very few readers will be interested in reading her "poetic adventures about nature."

nr   Mullen, Alicia Régoli de. Una naranja: el mundo. (Buenos Aires: Editorial Guadalupe, 1975. 168p.) Gr. adult.

An Argentinean housewife and mother briefly describes her childhood memories and then devotes many
pages to long, wearisome descriptions of her feelings as
a mother upon the birth of several of her children and
her housekeeping chores. There are also tedious references to her grocery shopping activities, her children's
first day in school and her feelings about God.

nr Murillo, José. Mi amigo el pespir. (Buenos Aires:
    Editorial Guadalupe, 1975. 190p.) Gr. 7-9.

An Argentinean author, who loves nature, wrote this
collection of animal stories to show young readers the
customs of animals in complete freedom. Unfortunately,
the complex vocabulary and long detailed descriptions
make these stories appealing only to readers who love
animals and are willing to toil through this unattractively
presented book. It includes stories about Argentinean
birds, bears, bulls, cats, dogs and snakes.

nr Nervi, Ricardo J. Tristán y la calandria. Illus:
    Viviana Barletta. (Buenos Aires: Editorial Plus Ultra,
    1977. 94p.) Gr. 7-10.

Pretentious collection of nine stories that are too
long and boring. The affected vocabulary and unnatural
situations described will certainly not appeal to young
readers. The stories' themes, which include the death
of a bird, a picture of a man, the soul of a bird, the
fire-fighter, etc., are overdone and lifeless.

m Ocampo. Silvina. El tobogán. Illus: Beatriz Bolster.
   (Buenos Aires: Angel Estrada, 1975. 18p.) Gr. 1-3.

Patricia recounts her adventures from things she
found in a magical toboggan: shoes to fly in the garden,
visits to strange countries, and bicycle rides from high
mountain tops. Attractive color illustrations simplify
the confusing, difficult-to-follow text.

m Poletti, Syria. Reportajes supersónicos. Illus: Uilar.
   (Buenos Aires: Editorial Sigmar, 1972. 45p.) Gr. 3-
   6.

Lilín, a five-year-old girl from Buenos Aires,
wishes she had a yard with trees, flowers, and animals
to play with. For her birthday she got a tape recorder
because her parents and aunt couldn't afford to buy her

a yard. Lilín proceeds to interview different people
with her new tape recorder: astronauts, Aztec people,
salmons, turtles, Noel and others. Unfortunately,
the extended descriptions and complicated incidents make
this an unappealing story for young children.

nr   Ramallo, José Antonio C.   Juan José en el país de las
hormigas. (Buenos Aires: Editorial Plus Ultra, 1975.
123p.) Gr. 7-12.

Fictionalizing daily life in an anthill, the author
writes with the intention of educating the reader about
ants and, especially, to preach his philosophy of love
towards humanity and hate towards war. The author describes ants as the most intelligent creatures of creation
and then continues to condemn man for the fission of the
atom, for creating slavery, for preparing for war, etc.
He ends his endless moralizing with a long message to
human beings about prosperity and peace.

nr   _____. El pato correntino que se fué a la luna.
(Buenos Aires: Editorial Plus Ultra, 1976. 121p.) Gr.
6-8.

Upon the request of his loved one the beautiful Black
Duck, an adventurous duck decides to go to the moon to
bring back a stone as a gift. Long, complicated descriptions tell about Patin's escapades in Buenos Aires, an
American farm, Cape Kennedy, the moon, and his return
to Earth where Black Duck had married someone else.
But, White Duck also loved him and they lived happily
ever after. A dull, educational story about two little
pigs that learned to be "model" children follows. They
learned not to fight among themselves and to be "good."

m   Requeni, Antonio. El pirata malapata. Illus: Raul
Fortin. (Buenos Aires: Editorial Plus Ultra, 1976.
45p.) Gr. 3-6.

This is a collection of eleven stories about pirates,
animals, clowns, and jungles with long, lifeless descriptions. The attractive, bold illustrations may interest
some children, but no child will want to plod through the
long text.

m   Roa Bastos, Augusto. El pollito de fuego. Illus: Juan
Marchesi. (Buenos Aires: Ediciones de la Flor, 1976.
28p.) Gr. 1-3.

A fire-damaged chick has the attention of a group
of children, although nobody agrees how this happened.
Long, complicated text describes the misadventures of
Pipiolín as it tried to make new friends with the many
people who were attracted by its strange condition. Unfortunately Pipiolín was very lonely and only after it
killed a bad viper was it loved by all the children. A
few attractive illustrations are the best part of this confusing story.

m   Salotti, Martha A.   Un viaje a la luna y otros cuentos.
    (Buenos Aires: Editorial Guadalupe, 1974.   46p.)   Gr.
    3-6.

    Attractive black-and-white illustrations but a slow-
    moving text detracts from these stories with simple vo-
    cabulary.   The themes of the stories (the moon, animals,
    winter) are appealing, but not much happens and the
    reader loses interest.

*   Schultz de Mantovani, Fryda.   Una gata como hay pocas.
    Illus: Raúl Fortin.   (Buenos Aires: Angel Estrada,
    1977.   18p.)   Gr. 2-4.

    Attractive illustrations complement the story of a
    cat and his growing family.   The youngest cat wanted to
    be a princess and the father educated her to be one.
    Unfortunately the text is a little too long and confusing,
    but the charming story of the princess-cat with revolu-
    tionary ideas that finally became queen might appeal to
    young readers with a good knowledge of Spanish.

nr Solves, Hebe.   Cuentos casi reales.   Illus: Amalia
    Cernadas.   (Buenos Aires: Editorial Plus Ultra, 1975.
    85p.)   Gr. 6-8.

    Monotonous collection of eight long stories about a
    magic donkey, a flying flower, air planets, a mysterious
    strainer, a lost note, and an endless cloth.   Extended
    descriptions that seem never to end and lifeless charac-
    ters result in tedious reading.

nr Tibaudin, Aldo.   La alcancía de los sueños.   Illus:
    Silvia Baldessari.   (Buenos Aires: Rosaló, 1967.   70p.)
    Gr. 4-8.

    Collection of six stories that include an "authentic
    moral lesson. "   Even though the themes might appeal to

younger children (fairies, circus, teddy bears, etc.) the long and difficult text is more appropriate for older readers. But the undisguised lessons in morality certainly detract from the enjoyment of these stories. The stories stress repentance, good work habits, self-reliance, and other attitudes that "good" children should demonstrate.

nr Vega, Adriana. La chinchilla maravilla. Illus: Chacha.
(Buenos Aires: Editorial Plus Ultra, 1977. 46p.) Gr.
3-6.

Wearisome collection of eighteen stories and poems about flowers, bunnies, balloons, dreams, etc. that could interest children if only the text could be drastically reduced. Some of the themes are basically amusing, but the long, boring descriptions will surely seem prohibitive to young readers.

nr Vettier, Adela. Cinco diálogos fantásticos. Illus:
Juan R. Carvajal. (Buenos Aires: Conjunta Editores,
1977. 92p.) Gr. 7-9.

Collection of five "fantasy" dialogues that will not interest young readers because of their heavy philosophizing about life, love, marriage, youth, death, time, and happiness. Vague thoughts stress the author's beliefs about a moral life through reminiscences and subtle sermons. Stilted illustrations pretend to decorate the dialogues.

m   Walsh, María Elena. Angelito. Illus: Jorge R.
Serrano. (Buenos Aires: Angel Estrada y Cía, 1974.
20p.) Gr. K-3.

Colorful illustrations and fast-moving text tell the story of Juancito, a naughty boy, who became good when he met his guardian angel. The angel is first seen in the sky observing Juancito's misbehavior on the earth. Saint Peter then sends the angel on his dangerous mission in a flying saucer to conceal the angel's identity.

m   _____. Cuentopos de Gulubú. (Buenos Aires: Editorial Sudamericana, 1975. 86p.) Gr. 4-8.

Collection of sixteen short stories with amusing illustrations that will appeal to readers with a good knowl-

edge of Spanish. Difficult vocabulary and complicated
situations limit these stories; the variety of themes, such
as Eskimo children, traditional stories retold in sarcastic style, and nonsense words make this collection of interest to a few sophisticated Spanish readers.

m   . Dailan Kifki. Illus: Vilar. (Buenos Aires:
Editorial Sudamericana, 1976. 177p.) Gr. 6-9.

An adventurous elephant, Dailan Kifki, causes amusing controversy in the home of a teenage girl who found
it in her front door in Buenos Aires. The clever illustrations and witty dialogue might entertain a few young
readers, but the long descriptions (forty-eight chapters)
might result in monotonous situations to most readers.
Selected chapters could be entertaining to teenagers.

*   . El diablo inglés. Illus: Raúl Fortin.
(Buenos Aires: Angel Estrada y Cía, 1974.   16p.) Gr.
2-5.

Delightful illustrations and charming text tell the
story of the English devils that appeared in Argentina in
1806.   Tomás, an Argentinean young man, is scared by
the appearance of an English soldier, who he confused
with the devil.   Tomás consults his friend, the witch
Manuela, who agrees with his fears.   This is a witty
story that alludes to the English invasion of Argentina
in 1806.

*   . El país de la geometría.   Illus: Néstor Luis
Battagliero.   (Buenos Aires: Editorial Estrada, 1974.
18p.) Gr. 3-6.

Amusing story which uses geometric designs and illustrations about the King of the Compass who was un-
happily searching for his round flower.   Simple dialogues
and charming illustrations engage the reader into geometric concepts.

*   . El reino del revés.   (Buenos Aires: Editorial Sudamericana, 1969.   97p.) Gr. 3-6.

Another good example of this author's attractive
rhymes for children.   She uses the same appealing line
illustrations and themes as in her other books.   "En una
cajita de fósforos" (pp. 40-41), a child describes her

fondness for her collection of treasures, such as buttons, sticks, pencils, and rags, which adults will never understand.

*   . La sirena y el capitán. Illus: Mirtha Castillo. (Buenos Aires: Angel Estrada, 1974. 18p.) Gr. 3-6.

Entertaining story with colorful illustrations of a beautiful mermaid captured by a Spanish captain. The captain wanted to marry the mermaid, but when the mermaid rejected him, he tied her to the trunk of a tree. The mermaid was saved by her friends, the animals of the forest, who attacked the captain.

*   . Zoo loco. (Buenos Aires: Editorial Sudamericana, 1970. 18p.) Gr. 3-6.

Excellent short limericks with simple vocabulary and appealing illustrations about zoo animals. A few pertain directly to Argentina, which make them an excellent introduction to that country. Others discuss animals in Ecuador and around Caracas, but most show animals that all children know.

m Yunque, Alvaro. Nuestros muchachos. (Buenos Aires: Editorial Plus Ultra, 1976. 78p.) Gr. 6-10.

Collection of ten fast-moving stories that realistically describe life in modern Buenos Aires. The variety of the themes and the brevity of the stories might make them more appealing to young readers, despite the philosophizing intent of the author. By using emotionally strong themes such as anti-semitism, "hippies," kidnappings, alcoholic mothers, etc. , the author pretends to teach moral lessons to adolescents.

LEGENDS

m Jijenu Sanchez, Rafael. De oir y contar. (Buenos Aires: Librería Hachette, S. A. 1960. 140p.) Gr. 3-12.

Amusing collection of popular legends, stories, riddles, proverbs, and rhymes from Spain, Argentina, Nicaragua, Chile, Puerto Rico, Colombia, Mexico, Peru,

Venezuela, Dominican Republic and El Salvador. Readers will especially enjoy "La semana" (p. 33), "Los tres estornudos" (p. 57), "El real y medio" (p. 61), "Dos cartas muy curiosas" (p. 64), and "El sabor de los refranes" (p. 96).

nr Ramallo, José Antonio. Cuentos y leyendas de la tierra misionera. (Buenos Aires: Editorial Plus Ultra, 1976. 187p.) Gr. 9-12.

Monotonous collection of twelve Argentinean animal legends that have been spoiled by the author through complex vocabulary, tedious descriptions and pretentious dialog. Cluttered illustrations do not add to the presentation of this book, or to the reader's interest.

m Schultz de Mantovani, Fryda. Leyendas argentinas. (Madrid: Aguilar, 1964. 39p.) Gr. 7-10.

Although the author states in the prologue that she "talks" to children eleven to thirteen years old, I am truly amazed at her choice of complex, long descriptions and sophisticated vocabulary. In the introduction to the legend "La maldonada" she writes: "... contemplaba con ojos tristes en qué habían venido a parar los sueños durante la larga travesía por el mar inhóspito, cuando, en demanda de honra y provecho se encaminaba a tierras tan australes como estas, que la había deparado la merced del Rey y Emperador Carlos V" (p. 7). Only an adult with a devoted interest in the Spanish language and Argentinean legends will enjoy reading this collection. Some of the legends have a genuine appeal, but the author's elaborate manner has spoiled the enjoyment from these legends. Many emphasize a Catholic message. Two interesting legends that, if retold, might be used with children are "La maldonada" (pp. 7-10), and "El huaco rojo" (pp. 19-22). The illustrations and format are appealing, but unfortunately the author did not have young readers in mind as she wrote.

POETRY

nr Cifra, Alejandro. Las poesías de Mari Pepa. Illus: Viviana Barletta. (Buenos Aires: Editorial Plus Ultra, 1976. 95p.) Gr. 4-8.

The author wrote this collection of poems "to gladden

the hearts of children. " But, unfortunately, the author's choice of words, subject matter and length of the poems do not adapt to the interests of young readers. Only the illustrator had children in mind; the illustrations are childlike and gay.

nr Galimberti de Guacci, Haydee. Canto al amanecer. (Buenos Aires: Ediciones Baires, 1975. 84p.) Gr. 1-6.

Collection of fifty-six lethargic poems that are supposed to amuse pre-school and kindergarten children. A few simple drawings by four- and five-year old children do not improve the monotonous presentation and generally tedious poems about animals, toys and dreams, as well as three testimonials to well-known children's books.

* Hernandez, José. Martín Fierro. (Buenos Aires: Editorial Sigmar, 1963. 150p.) Gr. 9-12.

This is a condensed version of the well-known poem, Martín Fierro, for young adult readers. It includes short, explanatory notes of words or phrases that are difficult to understand. It describes Martín Fierro's life adventures and his sad and difficult experiences with strangers and Indians. The second part relates the exploits of his two sons. An example from the poem is: "Y no piensen los oyentes/ Que del saber hago alarde;/ he conocido, aunque tarde,/ sin haberme arrepentido/ que es pecado cometido/ el decir ciertas verdades" (p. 24). Attractive illustrations enhance the descriptions.

nr Vettier, Adela, and Nela Grisolía. Alfombra mágica. Illus: Roberto Broullon. (Buenos Aires: Editorial Plus Ultra, 1975. 75p.) Gr. 1-3.

Collection of thirty-three monotonous poems about things common to children that are too difficult for most young children to understand or too uninspiring for older children. The unappealing illustrations conform to the dull poems.

* Walsh, María Elena. Tutú Marambá. (Buenos Aires: Editorial Sudamericana, 1969. 97p.) Gr. 3-6.

Outstanding collection of simple poems and rhymes

of things common to all children: toys, animals, friends,
etc. Attractive line illustrations, witty situations and
simple vocabulary will be enjoyed by all children. Some
examples are: "El vendedor de sueños" (p. 34), "Pájaro
loco" (p. 38), and "nada más" (p. 56).

*   . Versos tradicionales para los cebollitas.
(Buenos Aires: Editorial Sudamericana, 1974. 139p.)
Gr. 4-8.

Outstanding collection of traditional Argentinean
rhymes and poems that will entertain readers with a
good knowledge of Spanish. The lack of illustrations
might negatively affect some young readers, but the
simple and amusing rhymes may be enjoyed by reading
them aloud.

SONGS

*   Pahlen, Kurt, and Juan B. Grosso. Música y canciones
para los más pequeños. (Buenos Aires: Kapelusz,
1973. 80p.) Gr. K-3.

Attractive illustrations and simple songs with music
of things common to young children: toys, days of the
week, rain, trees, animals, wind and "Cielito" (Baile
argentino, pp. 45-47) as an example of a popular
Argentinean song. The simple vocabulary and short
rhythms make this an outstanding addition to young children.

THEATER

*   Berdiales, Germán. Fábulas en acción para la escena
y para el aula. (Buenos Aires: Kapelusz, 1959. 84p.)
Gr. 6-8.

Well-known fables have been adapted for the stage
using simple characters and ending with the original
fable. Children who may need practice in fluency will
surely enjoy the short comedies with their added witty
moral. Some outstanding examples are "La cigarra y
la hormiga" (pp. 9-10), "El avaro que perdió su tesoro"
(pp. 51-53), and "La lechera" (pp. 27-28).

nr   . Felices vacaciones. (Buenos Aires:

Librería Hachette, S. A., 1959. 225p.) Gr. 7-adult.

Uninteresting collection of plays, poems and essays written for the purpose of "cultivating the children's minds during vacations." It includes monotonous religious legends and plays; dull plays about Christmas and fairy tales; spiritless essays about the sea and the mountains; and pretentious adaptations of stories by Anton Chekhov, Maxim Gorky, and Carlo Collodi.

*   . Teatro cómico para los niños. (Buenos Aires: Kapelusz, 1959. 172p.) Gr. 3-8.

Witty collection of eleven short comedies, ten dialogues, and fifteen monologues for children. The spirited action and simple vocabulary used throughout the selections make them attractive to listen to and are especially recommended for children who may want to practice short oral presentations. Of special interest may be the amusing comedy "La honradez" (pp. 11-14) and the short monologue "La edad feliz" (p. 129).

m   Medina, Enrique. Pelusa rumbo al sol. Illus: Norma Bonet. (Buenos Aires: Editorial Eskol, 1976. 90p.) Gr. 3-6.

Witty illustrations complement this educational, moralistic play about a ten-year-old shoeshine boy of Buenos Aires who wants to build a rocket to go to the sun. Nine characters are involved in the action, which is interesting at times, but ends in a highly moralizing tone about the "great sickness that affects humanity--fear."

nr   Zarri, Inés M. A. Candilejas infantiles. (Buenos Aires: Kapelusz, 1958. 164p.) Gr. 6-10.

Short moralistic plays for children's theater production that emphasize nationalism, Argentinean Independence, life in colonial Buenos Aires, and school holidays. The lack of illustrations and complicated text with long descriptions make this collection unappealing to young readers.

LEGENDS

m   Morales, Rafael. Leyendas del Caribe. (Madrid: Aguilar, 1972. 95p.) Gr. 9-12.

Attractive illustrations with, unfortunately, long and detailed descriptions of Caribbean legends make this collection dull and uninteresting to read. Religious indoctrination is emphasized: "Dios quiso salvar a unos pocos para que pudieran continuar predicando la verdadera religión entre los indios ... " (p. 41). The selection of stories and the illustrations are good, but to be used they should be retold to young listeners.

FICTION

nr   Allamand, Maité, and others. <u>El niño que fué</u>. II.
(Chile: Ediciones Nueva Universidad, 1975. 261p.)
Gr. 10-adult.

    Five Chilean authors were asked to contribute to the
second volume of these reminiscences in which "they
turn their eyes nostalgically to the time in which it was
more important to play than to occupy a distinguished
situation. " Unfortunately the affected style in which each
author narrates his early years results in lethargic reading of uninteresting remembrances. The other authors
that contributed to this edition are Julio Barrenechea,
Francisco Coloane, Carlos Ruiz-Tagle, and Roque Este-
ban Scarpa.

nr   Alonso, Carmen de. <u>Medallones de luna</u>. (Chile:
Publicaciones Infantiles Sociedad Editora, 1973. 98p.)
Gr. 3-6.

    Boring collection of five stories that are too long
and too slow to read. Perhaps the author intended these
stories to be read aloud to young children, but the small
black-and-white illustrations and the endless descriptions
will not hold the children's interest for long. Four are
innocuous animal stories and one is an adaptation of a
well-known fairy tale about a witch and a young girl.

m   _____. <u>Medallones de sol</u>. (Chile: Publicaciones
Infantiles Sociedad Editora, 1973. 90p.) Gr. 1-5.

    Collection of five amusing stories that were told to
the author by her grandmother and which might be used
to read aloud to children. The stories describe a sly
fox, a lazy servant, a clever dog, a frightened lion and
a kind prince. The constant excitement and fast-moving

action of these stories will appeal to young listeners,
despite the small number of black-and-white illustrations.

m   Barrios, Eduardo,   El niño que enloqueció de amor.
    (Chile: Editorial Nascimento, 1974. 118p.) Gr. 5-9.

    Chilean novel written in 1915 in which a boy con-
    fides his "passionate" young love to his diary. His be-
    loved is an older woman who happens to be a friend of
    the family. There is too much repetition of the author's
    feelings, but the simple, genuine expressions of a grow-
    ing boy might make some parts of this book interesting
    reading. It is written in a simple language.

nr Bombal, María Luisa, and others. El niño que fué.
    (Chile: Ediciones Nueva Universidad, 1975. 239p.)
    Gr. 10-adult.

    Six Chilean authors reminisce about their childhoods
    and through their experiences, they remember the places
    where they grew up. Long, detailed descriptions of
    their homes, their mothers, their towns, etc. result in
    an affected collection of obtuse thoughts, such as:
    "¿Dónde termina la infancia? Dónde la deja atrás la
    adolescencia, que entontece, la desdeña porque ansía la
    edad de hombre, ronca y fumadora, y dueña de una
    sonrisa que viene como de vuelta de todas las cosas?"
    (p. 156). The other Chilean authors who wrote about
    their childhood are: Juan Guzmán Cruchaga, Miguel
    Arteche, Hernan del Solar, Enrique Lafourcade and
    Roberto Sarah.

nr Brunet, Marta. Cuentos para Marisol. (Chile:
    Empresa Editora Zig-Zag, 1977. 175p.) Gr. 3-6.

    Unappealing collection of twenty saccharine animal
    stories whose affected writing style and lifeless charac-
    ters won't interest young readers. Cheap paper and no
    illustrations do not add much to these stories, which
    pretend to describe "children's feelings and motivations. "

nr Cosani, Esther. Cuentos a Beatriz. (Chile: Publica-
    ciones Infantiles Sociedad Editora, 1973. 97p.) Gr.
    3-6.

    Lethargic collection of eight stories about cherubs
    and guardian angels that are supposed to be based upon

the mischiefs and pranks of the author's children. Unfortunately long descriptions, difficult vocabulary, few
illustrations, etc. will not entice young readers to these
stories.

nr _____. Las desventuras de Andrajo. (Chile:
Publicaciones Infantiles Sociedad Editora, 1973. 123p.)
Gr. 3-6.

Ten stories tell the misadventures of Andrajo, a
vagabond, who married the king's daughter. The moral
of these stories is that pure and simple men are chosen
by God to teach love towards the humble and towards
nature. Very few black-and-white illustrations and complicated vocabulary make these stories uninteresting to
young children and lessons in morality are not appreciated by any reader.

* Grez, Vicente. Marianita. (Chile: Editorial
Nascimento, 1976. 200p.) Gr. 9-12.

Absorbing love story originally published in Chile in
1885 by a well-known Chilean author who excellently de-
picts Chilean society of the nineteenth century. Marianita, a simple rural girl, falls in love with Camilo, a
sophisticated young man from Santiago. Camilo's court-
ships and marriage-of-convenience to a wealthy city girl
are described in this easy-to-understand, romantic novel.
Teenagers will find love, wealth, and family relationships
portrayed in this fast-moving story.

nr Moore, Sylvia. Las andanzas de Pepita Canela. (Chile:
Publicaciones Infantiles Sociedad Editora, 1973. 109p.)
Gr. 3-6.

Monotonous rhymes tell the story of Pepita and her
dolls. Artificial writing style and pretentious vocabulary
describe the souls of the dolls and clowns as well as
the lakes and other characters in this story. Also unappealing are a few lessons in "good" moral behavior.

nr Morel, Alicia. La hormiguita cantora y el duende
melodía. (Chile: Publicaciones Infantiles Sociedad
Editora, 1973. 124p.) Gr. 3-6.

Monotonous collection of thirteen fantasy stories
about fairies, flowers, queens, stones, giants, locusts,

frogs and fireflies that include insipid rhymes and endless descriptions.   Perhaps the author intends these
stories to be read aloud to children, but the lack of
illustrations and other unappealing characteristics certainly will not add interest to young listeners.

nr _____. El increíble mundo de Llanca. (Chile:
Ediciones Universitarias de Valparaiso, 1977.   86p.)
Gr. 6-8.

Perhaps because the author tried very hard to per-
sonify animals and to express their "most intimate
secrets," the results are a collection of monotonous
animal stories about an aristocratic Dalmatian dog, a
fish-eating mongrel dog, and other well-known animals
of the city of Valdivia.   Innocuous animal stories that
will not interest too many readers.

* Paz, Marcela. Papelucho. Illus: Yola. (Chile:
Editorial Universitaria, 1974.   109p.) Gr. 4-8.

First book of the outstanding Papelucho series originally published in Chile in 1947.   A favorite of Chilean
young readers because of its natural style, Papelucho
exemplifies a normal boy and his ingenious thoughts and
desires.   Written in diary style, Papelucho tells about
his feelings toward his family, going on vacations, getting
into trouble at boarding school, breaking a leg, etc.
Truly delightful reading about a normal boy that will
amuse boys and girls.   Fluency in Spanish is important
to understand this series.

* _____. Papelucho casi huérfano. (Chile: Editorial
Universitaria, 1975.   89p.) Gr. 4-8.

As soon as Papelucho's parents inherited a lot of
money from a rich uncle, they decide to take a trip to
the United States.   Papelucho stays in Chile with an
aunt; for this reason he is almost an orphan.   In his
natural style, Papelucho tells about his sad feelings: he
feels abandoned by his parents, neglected by his aunt,
and unwanted even by gypsies.   Everything is wonderful
as soon as mother returns.

* _____. Papelucho detective. (Chile: Editorial
Universitaria, 1974.   120p.) Gr. 4-8.

Papelucho is under arrest but not in prison, or so

he writes to his mother.   His mother and father are
very excited because she is expecting another baby.
There are problems with the pregnancy, so she must
stay in bed.   Papelucho describes his feelings about a
new sister, as well as getting into trouble with his
friends.

*   . Papelucho: diario secreto de Papelucho y el
marciano. (Chile: Editorial Universitaria, 1976.   119p.)
Gr. 4-8.

In a secret diary Papelucho tells his feelings about
his Martian friend who moves in with him.   Papelucho's
father and mother tried to help, but secrecy is crucial.
After causing a great deal of excitement at home,
Papelucho recovers from "bronchopneumonia" but his
secret and the Martian knowledge he gained stays with
him.

*   . Papelucho en vacaciones.   (Chile: Editorial
Universitaria, 1974.   110p.)   Gr. 4-8.

In the author's naturally animated style, Papelucho
narrates his camping adventures with his father and
mother.   Family quarrels and misunderstandings as well
as Papelucho's pranks with his friends are pleasingly
described in another Papelucho book.

*   . Papelucho historiador.   (Chile: Editorial
Universitaria, 1974.   99p.)   Gr. 4-8.

Papelucho decides to rewrite the history of Chile so
that he may truly understand it.   Continuing the author's
marvelously simple and amusing writing style, the reader is exposed to the pre-Columbian Indians of Chile,
the Quechua; to the Spanish Conquistadores; to the Spanish Colonial Period; and to the heroes who won Chile's
independence.   A tremendous book to introduce young
readers to the history of Spanish-speaking countries.

*   . Papelucho: mi hermana Ji. (Chile: Editorial
Universitaria, 1976.   96p.)   Gr. 4-8.

In another delightful Papelucho book, a charming
boy describes his feelings about having a younger sister.
Refreshing childish behavior and natural dialogues show
the daily life of a Chilean family, especially the trials
of a boy with a sister who goes to nursery school.

* _____. Papelucho: mi hermano Hippie. (Chile:
Editorial Universitaria, 1975. 127p.) Gr. 4-8.

Adventures of Papelucho as he tries to help his
hippie brother, Javier, survive while Javier attempts to
save the world. It is written in a very light manner,
which may attract boys whose Spanish vocabulary is
quite extensive. The incidents with Papelucho's teacher
and new friend Chori, who had never attended school,
are amusing. Readers will need a strong knowledge of
Spanish to enjoy Javier's return to his middle-class,
old-fashioned family.

* _____. Papelucho misionero. (Chile: Editorial
Universitaria, 1975. 120p.) Gr. 4-8.

Papelucho's father decides to go to Africa to search
for diamonds. Even though mother is concerned about
Papelucho's and Javier's education, the family embarks
on flight 623 to Dakar, Senegal. In a witty, amusing
style Papelucho tells about flying on a plane, preparing
for an international trip, arriving in a new country,
failing to find any diamonds, and returning home.

* _____. Papelucho perdido. (Chile: Editorial
Universitaria, 1974. 95p.) Gr. 4-8.

During all the confusion at the train station,
Papelucho and his sister get on the wrong train going to
southern Chile. The many ingenious adventures that
Papelucho and his younger sister go through in trying to
locate their missing parents are again charmingly described. Several incidents show life on Chilean farms,
as viewed by a boy from the capital.

m _____. Papelucho: ¿Soy dix leso? (Chile: Editorial
Universitaria, 1974. 109p.) Gr. 4-8.

Papelucho narrates his adventures with a police
officer in trying to arrest a band of criminals. By
lightly discussing Papelucho's case of "dix lesia"
(dyslexia) the author tries to convey confidence to the
children and their parents about their "problem." The
story's easy-going, natural manner will be enjoyed by
readers with a good knowledge of Spanish, even though
Papelucho's reading disability (dyslexia) is never explained.

m _____. Los pecosos. (Chile: Ediciones Universitarias de Valparaiso, 1976. 176p.) Gr. 6-8.

Fast-moving story about six children that describes a multitude of childish mischiefs. The human characterization of the six children and the amusing dialogue will be enjoyed by young readers. Unfortunately, the activities and anecdotes told in the story are about children approximately eight to ten years old, and yet the vocabulary and length of the book (176 pages) might be more appealing to children eleven through thirteen. Good addition for fluent Spanish readers.

nr Prado, Pedro. Alsino. (Chile: Nascimento, 1973. 263p.) Gr. 10-adult.

Interminable descriptions of the author's feelings about nature and his surroundings make this novel of 263 pages written in 1920 a long exercise in constant, detailed accounts of the dawn, silent summers, a song of love, solitude, etc. This is a tedious novel, impossible to enjoy.

m Rojas, Manuel. Hijo de ladrón. (Chile: Editorial Quimantu Limitada, 1973. 312p.) Gr. 10-adult.

This novel is considered one of the most important Chilean works of fiction. The narrator remembers his childhood and youth as the son of the thief, El Gallego, by relating the sorrow and pain of poverty and humiliation. In spite of the anxieties of life in prison, loneliness, hunger and lack of work the author states that his childhood was not disagreeable, but full of passionate happenings. Interesting novel that may be enjoyed by adventurous readers who are thoroughly at home in the Spanish language.

nr _____. Mares libres y otros cuentos. (Chile: Ediciones Universitarias de Valparaiso, 1975. 146p.) Gr. 10-adult.

Even though this collection of short stories was selected especially for young adult readers, I truly wonder if any sophisticated reader might begin to understand, let alone enjoy, these stories that show "the solidarity of the humble, the dignity of the most desperate situations, the tireless search of new structures in

relationship to man's torn existence, the purifying ascet-
icism of language, etc. " Only mature readers who are
interested in reading Chilean "superealistic" authors
should try this collection of amorphous stories.

nr Tejeda, Juan.   Cuentos de la selva.   (Chile:
Publićaciones Infantiles Sociedad Editora, 1973.   98p.)
Gr. 3-6.

Sluggish collection of six animal stories about a cat
who wanted to be king, a cat who didn't become a king,
a serpent and a flea, a businesslike wolf, zebras and
dragons, narrated in a very slow-moving style.   The
underscored message is that "one must always have
happiness in one's heart and then everything results all
right. "   The themes of these stories are for younger
children, but the long descriptions certainly will not
appeal to them.

HISTORY

nr Medina, José Toribio.   El piloto Juan Fernández.
(Chile: Editora Nacional Gabriela Mistral, 1974.   258p.)
Gr. 9-adult.

This is a highly-documented historical narration of
the people and times that influenced the conquest of
Chile, originally published in 1918.   The strict enumer-
ation of facts makes this book of special interest to historians, because of its technical and well-researched information.   It describes the life and the accomplishments
of Juan Fernández and Juan Jufre.   Many footnotes and
ten copies of original sixteenth-century colonial documents
make this a valuable contribution to scholarly Chilean
historians.

LEGENDS

m Alonso, Carmen de.   Cantaritos o leyendas americanas.
(Chile: Publicaciones Infantiles Sociedad Editora, 1973.
83p.) Gr. 7-12.

Collection of seven legends from Cuba, Venezuela,
Paraguay, the United States, Haiti, Argentina and Chile
written in an affected style that detracts from the sim-

plicity of the original legends.   Good readers of Spanish
may enjoy reading these well-known legends despite the
author's choice of difficult words and an unnecessary poem at the beginning and end of each legend.

*   Campos Menéndez. Enrique.   Sólo el viento.   (Chile:
     Editora Nacional Gabriela Mistral, 1973.   158p.)   Gr.
     9-adult.

     Remarkable collection of twelve Chilean legends
from ancient Ona origin (an extinguished pre-Columbian
Indian race that inhabited Tierra del Fuego until the late
1800's), written in a simple, fast-moving style.   The
legends tell about the peoples' dreams, customs and
desires as well as Ona's marriage celebrations, family
traditions and problems with the white men.

POETRY

nr   Jara Azócar, Oscar.   Operación alegría.   (Chile:
     Editorial Andres Bello, 1969.   99p.)   Gr. 4-8.

     Unattractive collection of poems and supposed nurs-
ery rhymes written by the author for pre-schoolers
about complex philosophical ideas, such as the fullness
of life, the gratitude of children, the appreciation of
friendship, the loyalty of animals, the happiness of
studying, etc.   I've never met a child who is enter-
tained by such concepts, or who can understand such
complicated vocabulary.

nr   Romero, María, editor.   Los mejores versos para
     niños.   (Chile: Publicaciones Infantiles Sociedad Editora,
     1974.   216p.)   Gr. 4-adult.

     Even though the editor states that these poems were
ultimately selected by children, I truly doubt that any
child or young adult will ever read these poems for enjoyment.   The editor hopes that these poems will be
useful in homes or schools "to help in the formation of
the young soul by exalting love towards God, country,
parents, schools, and nature. "   These poems are in-
comprehensible to children and wearisome in their
efforts to enlighten young adults.

SONGS

* Pérez Ortega, Juan. <u>Música folklórica y popular infantil</u> <u>chilena.</u> (Chile: Ediciones Universitarias de Valparaíso, <u>1976.</u> 282p.) Gr. 10-adult.

Outstanding scholarly collection of Chilean popular and folkloric music for children that includes songs, nursery rhymes, games and ballads. For each melody the author has added a musical description, the words of the song, and a brief history of the piece. Music teachers will find a delightful amount of information that could be useful to children or adults.

COLOMBIA

BIOGRAPHY

m Caballero Calderón, Eduardo. Memorias infantiles.
(Colombia: Editorial Bedout, 1964. 251p.) Gr. 10-
adult.

A well-known Colombian author writes down his
childhood memories of the period between the years 1916
and 1924. He offers interesting glimpses of life in a
Colombian hacienda during the early 1920's, such as the
importance and influence of the Catholic religion, the
role of servants, the deep mourning customs, and the
strong feelings toward family members. This autobiog-
raphy might interest students whose Spanish vocabulary
is very extensive and who are particularly interested in
life in a Colombian hacienda.

FICTION

nr Bonilla-Naar, Alfonso, and others. Lucero--cuento de
Navidad y otros cuentos infantiles. (Colombia:
Instituto Colombiano de Cultura, 1971. 102p.) Gr. 7-8.

Six incredibly obtuse stories about God, nature and
patriotism--written by Alfonso Bonilla-Naar, Rafael
Jaramillo Arango, Santiago Pérez Triana and Fanny
Osorio--which cannot possibly be enjoyed by young readers because of their pretentious fantasy, dull and slow-
moving writing style, and moralistic teachings. The unattractive presentation and cheap paper will also keep
readers away.

m Caballero Calderón, Eduardo. El almirante niño.
(Madrid: Talleres Gráficos de Ediciones Castilla, 1953.
82p.) Gr. 9-12.

Three touching stories that recreate three different historical periods through the lives of famous men. "El almirante niño" describes Columbus through the eyes of his son. "El rey de Roma" shows Napoleon as a father and deposed emperor. "El caballito de Bolivar" flatters Bolivar as a liberator and horseman.

nr García Mejía, Hernando. Rosa de Navidad. (Colombia: Ediciones Acuarimantima, 1974. 68p.) Gr. 6-8.

Uninspired, slow-moving story that preaches to the readers through the thoughts of the Three Wise Men and Santa Claus about the evils of playing with toy guns and other toy weapons. They insist that for Christmas children should only receive "something that educates them and reminds them of peace." The author ends the story with a long sermon about man's destructive nature and what the author believes is man's salvation.

m Isaacs, Jorge. María. (Barcelona: Editorial Labor, 1970. 362p.) Gr. 9-adult.

Considered by many critics and educators as the representative and most popular South American novel, María is the touching love story of María and Efraín. It has marvelous descriptions of life in rural Colombia in the 1860's as well as sentimental expressions of the author's feelings about his family and his country. This novel will provide an emotional historical background to family values, slaves in South American haciendas, and the role of women in the nineteenth century as perceived by a romantic author of the period. Excellent for romantics with a good knowledge of Spanish.

nr Pombo, Rafael. Fábulas y verdades. (Colombia: Editorial Bedout, 1974. 306p.) Gr. 7-12.

Wearisome collection of 273 fables and moralistic stories that pretend to exalt the reader by "educating" him about the value of life, education of women, patriotism, generosity, etc. Tedious reading that bores by its constant moralizing.

POETRY

nr Osorio, Fanny. Lección de poesía. (Colombia: Biblioteca Colombiana de Cultura, 1971. 119p.) Gr. 4-8.

Even though the introduction of this dull anthology states that these poems were "carefully selected for children's recreation," I truly wonder if any child will even enjoy a single one of these poems. Monotonously they moralize about God, love of country, heroes, honor, etc. Hopefully no child will be exposed to such dull poems as these.

RELIGIOUS STORIES

nr Caballero Calderón, Eduardo. La historia en cuentos. (Madrid: Talleres Gráficos de Ediciones Castilla, 1953. 79p.) Gr. 4-8.

Three biblical religious stories which are "La estrella de Ismael," which describes the birth of God in Belén, "La hija de Jairo," which tells of the coming of the Messiah, and "La Pasión segun la hija de Jairo," a story about the crucifixion of Christ. The obvious intent of these stories is to indoctrinate readers about the value of religious beliefs.

nr García Mejía, Hernando. Cuento para soñar. (Colombia: Editorial Bedout, S. A. , 1973. 155p.) Gr. 4-8.

Moralistic story that hopes "to teach young readers the science of love. " In a monotonous style, it describes Darín, "como todos los niños buenos, estudiaba y era un buen escolar, a pesar de la pobreza" [like all good children, he studied and was a good student, in spite of his poverty] (p. 18). Innumerable miracles are narrated that prove Darín's basic goodness, with the story's moral: man should never forget God.

THEATER

nr Rodríguez, Julia. Biombo infantil. (Colombia: Instituto Colombiano de Cultrua, 1974. 78p.) Gr. 3-6.

Collection of five dull children's plays that are recommended by the author to be performed with puppets. The unattractive presentation, slow-moving action, and stale characters will not make this book appealing to young readers.

COSTA RICA

FICTION

nr Centeno Guell, Fernando. Fábula del bosque. Illus:
Juan Manuel Sánchez. (Costa Rica: Editorial Costa
Rica, 1976. 79p.) Gr. 6-8.

The author pretends to amuse young readers through
his poetic interpretation of life in the forest. Each forest animal and plant explains its important functions and
characteristics through conversations with other animals
and plants. Perhaps a few sections of this book will
maintain the readers' interest, but it becomes monotonous
reading after a few animals. Five black-and-white, simple line illustrations are not enough to illustrate an animal book for children.

m Fallas, Carlos Luis. Mamita Yunai. (Costa Rica:
Librería Lehmann, 1977. 222p.) Gr. 10-adult.

The first novel of the great Costa Rican writer,
Carlos Luis Fallas, originally published in 1940, is a
result of the author's political work. It describes the
author's sad impressions and experiences in the banana
plantations of the United Fruit Company in Costa Rica.
It is a strong indictment against "the Yanqui imperialists"
and American business practices as viewed by the author.
The political character of this novel, as well as the complicated vocabulary, make it difficult reading for most
young adults.

m _____. Marcos Ramírez--Aventuras de un muchacho.
(Costa Rica: Librería Lehmann, 1976. 299p.) Gr.
10-adult.

Considered by many critics the outstanding Costa
Rican novel, Marcos Ramírez is the Tom Sawyer of the
Costa Rican people. It describes the adventures and

35

constant mischief of a young boy who grew up in a typical Costa Rican home of the poorer classes. In a spontaneous, realistic style the author relates his early years
and his mother's influence in his life, the cities where
he went to school, and the poverty of the Costa Rican
farmer. There are also a few references to the powerful influences of the United Fruit Company in Costa Rica.
Fluent, mature readers of Spanish will certainly enjoy
this human view of a Costa Rican youth, but the long
text and sophisticated vocabulary might make it difficult
reading for the average teenager.

*   Gagini, Carlos. Cuentos y otras prosas. (Costa Rica:
      Librería Lehmann, 1969. 84p.) Gr. 9-12.

      Remarkable collection of fourteen short stories and
four essays by the well-known Costa Rican author,
Gagini, who originally published them in the 1920's.
The brevity and conciseness of these stories as well as
the realism described make them fascinating reading.
They are also a marvelous introduction to the life of
Costa Rican people of the early twentieth century. Fluent
readers of Spanish will be enchanted by the human lives
portrayed in these stories.

m   García Monge, Joaquín. El Moto. (Costa Rica:
      Librería Lehmann, 1977. 48p.) Gr. 10-adult.

      This most widely read novel by adolescents in Costa
Rica was originally published in 1900. The main theme
of this brief novel is helplessness. The young man,
Moto, is an orphan who falls in love with Cundila, a
submissive daughter who has agreed to marry her par-
ent's choice. Moto is a poor, honest, hard-working
peasant, but his values are not appreciated by Cundila's
parents. She married Don Sebastian, the town's wealthy
patriarch, thirty years older than Cundila. Complicated
vocabulary and difficult-to-understand colloquialisms
make this novel appropriate reading only for those fluent
in Spanish. Although brevity is indeed a delightful in-
centive in this novel.

NON-FICTION

*   Salguero, Miguel (pseud. for Miguel Zúñiga Diaz). Así
      vivimos los Ticos. (Costa Rica: Editorial Universitaria
      Centroamericana, 1976. 395p.) Gr. 9-12.

Outstanding collection of twenty-three interviews
that describes the ways of thinking and living of a great
variety of Costa Rican people.   In a very honest and
amusing manner, the people respond to many personal
questions relating to their work and daily living habits.
Some of the people interviewed are a poor peasant, a
construction worker, a bank clerk, a rural teacher, a
prostitute, a Catholic priest, a university student, a
minister of state and many others.   Remarkable journal-
istic report that reflects the thoughts and feelings of the
people of Costa Rica.

POETRY

m   Ríos, Lara. Algodón de azúcar. (Costa Rica:
     Editorial Costa Rica, 1976. 82p.) Gr. 2-5.

     Collection of thirty-three poems for children about
animals, grandma's slippers, at the zoo, friends, Costa
Rica, nonsense, candy, etc. , written in a simple, easy-
to-understand language.   The bold illustrations were done
by elementary children, but unfortunately only a few are
in color.   The length of these poems may cause problems
to readers who are not fluent in Spanish.

nr   Sáenz, Carlos Luis. El viento y Daniel. (Costa Rica:
     Editorial Costa Rica, 1976. 80p.) Gr. 6-8.

     Collection of fifty-four affected poems for children
that were written by the author to enrich the young
readers' sensitivities and to compensate for the violence
and ugliness that children receive through the mass
media.   Unfortunately these poems will not appeal to
young readers because of their unnatural writing style
and abstract ideas.

CUBA

BIOGRAPHY

* Abreu Gómez, Ermilo. Juárez. (Cuba: Instituto
Cubano del Libro, 1971. 48p.) Gr. 4-8.

Excellent biography of Benito Pablo Juárez that describes in simple-to-understand language his early years
in Oaxaca, his education, his political beliefs, and his
outstanding contributions to Mexico: "Las leyes de
reforma," his constant fight for Mexico's freedom, and
the most extensive educational reform movement. Despite the simple black-and-white illustrations and mediocre presentation, this biography highlights the achievements of a great Mexican hero who is also known as "el
Benemérito de las Américas."

* El Niño Bach [no author given]. Illus: Montserrat
Clavé. (Cuba: Instituto Cubano del Libro, 1971. 58p.)
Gr. 6-10.

Excellent biography of Juan Sebastián Bach which
narrates interesting episodes of his youth. Written in a
simple, dynamic style it shows Bach's love for music
and his dedication to his studies and practice of all
musical instruments. Pleasing illustrations make this
an enjoyable biography of the great musical composer of
the eighteenth century.

FICTION

m Abreu Gómez, Ermilo. Canek. Illus: Monserrat Clavé.
(Cuba: Instituto Cubano del Libro, 1973. 70p.) Gr.
7-12.

A "poem in prose" written by the Mexican author
Ermilo Abreu Gómez which tries to reflect the sorrow,

38

injustice and poverty of the Mayan Indians of Yucatan
through the story of Canek, the legendary Mayan hero.
The excellent presentation and striking illustrations add
appealing touches to this difficult-to-read novel about
liberty, injustice, death, God, war, etc.

nr Fortes de la Osa, Mercedes; Teresita Rodríguez-Baz;
and Elena G. Lavin. Cuentos para tí. (Cuba:
Instituto Cubano del Libro, 1974. 126p.) Gr. 4-8.

Collection of fifteen insipid stories which won children's literature awards in Cuba in 1972. Long descriptions about animals, flowers and toys are interspersed
with patriotic and moralistic teachings to form wearisome, slow-moving stories.

m González, Celedonio. La soledad es una amiga que
vendrá. (Florida: Ediciones Universal, 1971. 95p.)
Gr. 9-12.

Short essays written in Miami, Florida, by a Cuban
that describe the author's feelings about his arrival to
the United States. The simple sentences and witty sense
of humor would make them enjoyable reading to young
adults. In the essay "La fuga," Juan Antonio responds
to a dog that bit him: "El perro, doctor, era comunista
y se guedó en Cuba" (p. 20). The author also expresses
bitterness and resentment about his new life in the United
States: "Es culpable del error de los errores, cual huir
de un sistema totalitario que imperaba en su patria--
según dicen--para venir a vivir a la Democracia Ameri-
cana. El que hace eso ... tiene indiscutiblemente que
ir a formar parte del grupo de los retrasados mentales"
(p. 28). He is sarcastic about his new peaceful existence and his job in a factory (p. 34); "La mesa" (p.
51), tells about Russians in Cuba; and "La estatura,"
especially on page 76, discusses Fidel Castro and the
Cuban revolution from a questioning perspective.

nr Hernandez Costales, Elsa. La niña de mi cuento.
Illus: Muñoz Bachs. (Cuba: Instituto Cubano del
Libro, 1972. 79p.) Gr. K-8.

Collection of nine stories that won children's literature awards in Cuba in 1972. "Flores, miel y oro" is
the only one that might interest young readers, grades
4-8, because of its action and adventure during Spanish

Colonial times in Cuba. The other stories abound in long descriptions about animals and people, but nothing seems to happen. Most of the stories add a commonplace moral at the end.

nr   Hernandez-Miyares, Julio, editor. Narradores cubanos de hoy. (Florida: Ediciones Universal, 1975. 78p.) Gr. 9-12.

Eleven Cuban authors who are now exiled in the United States, Spain and Venezuela contributed to this collection of twenty-two short stories. The complicated narrations with complex vocabulary make them difficult to comprehend. Perhaps only adults who are used to long, abstract descriptions will enjoy these stories. Some of the authors represented are Concepción T. Alzola, Fausto Masó, Carlos Alberto Montaner and José Sánchez Baudy.

nr   Hudson, Guillermo Enrique. Allá lejos y hace tiempo. (Cuba: Instituto Cubano del Libro, 1973. 225p.) Gr. 7-8.

The author writes about his early years in minute, tedious details in this book which was first published in 1918. He elaborates upon his first house in Argentina, the trees he loved, the teachers he hated, and countless, dull, occurrences that surrounded his youth.

nr   Murillo, José, and Ana María Ramb. Renanco y los ultimos huemules. Illus: Manuel del Toro. (Cuba: Instituto Cubano del Libro, 1976. 216p.) Gr. 6-8.

Through the eyes of a grandfather deer, the reader is exposed to long, endless descriptions of life in the forest. Forest animals describe their feelings about death, life, human beings, etc. Several two-tone deer illustrations serve as decorations and to break up the 216 pages of boring text.

*   Robés Masses, Ruth, and Herminio Almendros. Había una vez .... (Cuba: Instituto Cubano del Libro, 1971. 189p.) Gr. 2-6.

Very good collection of fifty-two well-known fairy tales, riddles, and poems written in a simple, easy-to-understand style that will be enjoyed by young readers

or listeners. Despite the mediocre illustrations and
cheap paper, the charm of the fairy tales has been very
well preserved. Some of the tales included in this collection are "Los tres cerditos," "Caperucita roja," "El
gato con botas," "Cenicienta," "Blanca nieve" and many
others.

m   Rodriguez, Félix Pita. Niños de Viet Nam. (Cuba:
    Instituto Cubano del Libro, 1974. 105p.) Gr. 4-10.

    Long political stories written for the purpose of
showing that "Vietnamese children paid a hard tribute to
making tomorrow's world possible." The stories are a
strong condemnation of the United States and in violent
emotional language the author offers multiple examples
of the "barbarian American invasion" which destroyed
the land, bombarded schools, and killed children. The
author describes the children's "just" feelings of hate
against the "fascist Yankee pilots." Interesting reading
if only for the purpose of seeing political propaganda
written for children.

                          LEGENDS

*   Almendros, Herminio. Oros viejos. (Cuba: Instituto
    Cubano del Libro, 1974. 230p.) Gr. 5-10.

    Outstanding collection of thirty-eight legends from
North and South America, Europe, Asia, and Africa
which maintain their original flavor and ingenuity. Of
special interest are the well-known legends of the Aztecs,
Mayas (Mexico), Incas (Peru), Araucos (Chile), and
Guaraníes (Uruguay). This is an excellent introduction
to world cultures through the legends of its people written
in simple language and told in a dynamic style. One cannot help but wonder why the author decided to include
two political notes which seem uncalled for: China,
which "suffered pain and misery under the imperialist
exploitation ... has now reached an important place in
the progress of the history of the world" (p. 98).
Russia "is now the leader of the world's civilization"
(p. 144). But these are minor notes in a most attractive selection of the world's legends.

m   Alzola, Concepción T. La más fermosa. (Florida:
    Ediciones Universal, 1975. 85p.) Gr. 9-12.

A Cuban author who now lives in Maryland has collected Cuban legends.   The short introduction to each
legend offers a short historical glimpse to Cuba and its
culture.   Of special interest to young adults is "El conde
de Barreto" (pp. 41-44) which shows the division of
classes in Cuba: the white masters and the black slaves.

NON-FICTION

nr   Almendros, Herminio.   Cosas curiosas de animales.
(Cuba: Instituto Cubano del Libro, 1974.   78p.)   Gr.
7-12.

Lengthy descriptions of the life and migrations of
various animals written with too much detail and tedious
information.   Four pages of small print and commonplace illustrations portray the lives of the following animals: sea urchins, earthworms, bats, bees, locusts,
elephants, gorillas, birds of passage, eels, salmons,
and whales.

POETRY

nr   Aguirre, Mirta.   Juegos y otros poemas.   (Cuba:
Instituto Cubano del Libro, 1974.   98p.)   Gr. 3-12.

In the introduction to her book the author states that
she wrote this book for children from age five through
adolescence for their enjoyment.   Even though this book
is very attractively presented, with colorful designs, I
am afraid the author did not accomplish her purpose.
The poems, monotonous and uninspired, describe the
days of the week, water, and animals; in the section
"Island, " she offers florid tributes to Fidel Castro in
three of her poems.

m   Nuñez, Ana Rosa.   Escamas del Caribe (Haikus de Cuba).
(Florida: Ediciones Universal, 1971.   75p.)   Gr. adult.

Cuban author who is now exiled in the United States
writes poems about her native country, about nature and
about love.   Some of her poems may be enjoyed by older,
sophisticated readers who have deep feelings for Cuba;
otherwise her poems are too complex and abstract for
young readers.

FICTION

m   Benites Vinueza, Leopoldo.   Argonautas de la selva,
     Vol. I. (Ecuador: Publicaciones Educativas Ariel,
     1972? 168p.) Gr. 9-adult.

     Historical novel originally published in 1945 which
describes the adventures, mishaps, and misfortunes of
daring Spanish Conquistadores in discovering the Amazon
River in the sixteenth century. The first part is a long,
detailed narrative of the hunger, loneliness and ambition
that the Conquistadores experienced in their battles with
the Indians. The last few pages (162-168) are a fascinating account of the fierce female Amazon warriers
that conquered their neighbors through fear. It describes
the Amazons' mating habits in which: "El macho es para
ellas un instrumento de perpetución de la especie....
Pasado el ayuntamiento carnal, vuelven las guerreras a
su orgullosa soledad" (p. 164). No males were allowed
inside their walls after sunset. Boy babies were killed
and sent to their fathers' tribes and girl babies were
cherished and educated for war.

*   .   Argonautas de la selva, Vol. II. (Ecuador:
Publicaciones Educativas Ariel, 1972? 168p.) Gr. 10-
adult.

     Through the dreams of riches and conquest of a
Spanish adventurer of the sixteenth century, the reader
is exposed to the hopes and misfortunes of an unsuccessful campaign to conquer the Ecuadorian jungle. Orellana's
failure to obtain financial support from the Spanish or
Portuguese crowns, his losses during the hazardous sea
voyage, his love and devoted concern for his wife, the
hunger, thirst and sickness, and Orellana's defeat by
Indians in the New World make this novel an engrossing
adventure of broken dreams and unlimited ambition.

Spanish readers should find this novel to be a fascinating description of an unsuccessful expedition.

m   Mera, Juan León. Cumandá. (Ecuador: Publicaciones Educativas Ariel, 1974. 190p.) Gr. 10-adult.

The author of this well-known Ecuadorian novel is referred to as the father of Ecuadorian realism and Cumandá is known as his best "poetic novel. " Written in 1877, this novel describes the harsh jungles of eastern Ecuador and the conflicts and hatreds between the "savage native tribes" and the white Christian, through the unfortunate love affair of Cumandá and Carlos. The long, detailed descriptions of the jungle are balanced by a fast-moving text that includes brotherly love, racial hatred, and constant vengeance. Older, sophisticated readers might enjoy this romantic novel which immerses the reader in the life of Colonial Ecuador of the 1700's.

HISTORY

*   Buitrón, Aníbal. Taita Imbabura--vida indígena en los Andes. (Ecuador: Misión Andina del Ecudor, 1976? 101p.) Gr. 9-adult.

The life of the Otavalo Indians from Ecuador is interestingly described in this readable and informative narrative. The simple writing style does much to improve the unattractive paperback presentation. The book describes the Otavalo Indians' food, historical background, work habits, parties, clothing, daily life and many other customs. It is interesting to note the author's contrasting examples of the Otavalo's habits regarding work: "Los indios, hombres y mujeres, niños y adultos, empiezan a trabajar a las cinco de la mañana, " and drinking habits: "En general durante las fiestas los indios gastan todo el dinero ahorrado en el año, se emborrachan, pelean, son conducidos a las cárceles, pagan multas e inician juicios interminables. "

nr Calle, Manuel J. Leyendas del tiempo heroico. (Ecuador: Publicaciones Educativas Ariel, 1975. 174p.) Gr. 9-12.

Collection of historical scenes of Ecuador that were originally published in 1905. The author's purpose was to write "a book of readings that would describe to children the great days of Ecuador's Independence and would encourage them to further study that time in the history of Ecuador." The author tried to simplify the historical narrative, but reported the facts and dates with "scrupulous care." The exaggerated patriotic tone and the dates and laws reported make this book of interest only to scholars who wish to study a patriotic view of Simón Bolívar and other aspects of Ecuador's independence movement.

LEGENDS

m Gangotena y Jijón, Don Cristóbal. Al margen de la historia. (Ecuador: Editorial Casa de la Cultura Ecuatoriana, 1969. 193p.) Gr. 9-adult.

Collection of twenty-five legends originally published in Ecuador in 1923. The author collected these legends for the purpose of entertaining his readers through the folklore and legends of colonial Ecuador. Amusing situations of the daily life of Ecuador in the seventeenth and eighteenth centuries are described, such as nuns and convents, high-ranking gentlemen, and the love-life of well-known generals. The presentation and writing style of this book limit its appeal to studious Spanish readers.

POETRY

nr Carrera, Carlos. Nueva poesía infantil. (Ecuador: Ministerio de Educación, 1975. 98p.) Gr. 4-8.

The author wrote one hundred and sixty poems that express his feelings and thoughts about motherhood, Walt Disney, the moon, nature, dreams, people, etc. The stilted descriptions and artificial language of these poems result in one- man's personal expression of ideas, but these poems are certainly not for the enjoyment of young readers.

GUATEMALA

LEGENDS

nr Asturias, Miguel Angel. Leyendas de Guatemala. (Buenos Aires: Editorial Losada, 1957. 150p.) Gr. 7-12.

Even though Asturias is considered an outstanding Latin American author since obtaining the Nobel Prize in Literature in 1967, I do not believe he will be read and/or enjoyed by young adults. This collection of Guatemalan legends is overloaded with long detailed descriptions of nature and historical places. Too many words are used that interrupt the dynamic aspects of a legend. Perhaps only Asturias' admirers will feel the compulsion of plodding through his long, descriptive writing. It includes two essays and six legends.

MEXICO

ART

* Fernandez, Justino. El arte mexicano. (Middlesex, England: Hamlyn House, 1968. 125p.) Gr. 3-12.

The great Mexican historian and art critic, J. Fernandez, has put together an outstanding example of Mexico's artistic heritage through ceramics, pyramids, sculpture, palaces, convents, churches, colonial paintings and modern murals. The 59 excellent photographs in color show the pre-Columbian achievements of the Olmecs, Toltecs, Mayas and Aztecs, the Mexican architecture of the colonial period, and with the Revolution of 1910 the beginnings of Mexican mural painting.

FICTION

m Abreu Gómez, Ermilo. Canek. (México: Ediciones Oasis, 1972. 144p.) Gr. 9-12.

Novel which describes the sorrow, poverty and abuse of the Mayan Indians of Yucatan. It is the story of the legendary Mayan hero, Canek. Even though this novel is required reading for adolescents in Mexico, it is difficult to read, as it expresses the author's thoughts on liberty, injustice, death, God, war, etc.

* Altamirano, Ignacio M. La Navidad en las montañas. (México: Editorial Porrúa, 1972. 125p.) Gr. 9-12.

Religious novel which describes the author's memories of his town, his parents and brother during the happy Christmas celebrations of his youth in nineteenth-century rural Mexico.

nr Arroyo, Imelda Ramírez de. La cigarra fantástica.

(México: Fotoedisa, 1977. 47p.) Gr. 3-6.

Wearisome collection of nine long stories that abound in complicated descriptions of the gloomy feelings and thoughts of the main characters (mainly animals, such as fish, butterflies, birds, and flowers). Perhaps the author intended to inspire young readers through the benevolent actions of her characters, but the result is a tedious collection of spiritless stories.

m   Gutiérrez Zacarías, Flavio. Shunco. (México: Tipografía Tonantzín, 1972. 190p.) Gr. 9-12.

Novel which describes the traditions of ancient towns in Oaxaca where myth and the ancient world are mixed with reality.

m   Lizardi Fernandez, José Joaquin de. El periquillo sarniento. (México: Editorial Porrúa, 1972. 467p.) Gr. 9-12.

Long, moralistic, educational novel which examines the vices and virtues of nineteenth-century Mexican society. A schemer relates his life's adventures as an elementary student, as a university student and as a gambler.

m   Martínez Franco, Raimundo. Trikis Trikis. (México: Ediciones P. A. K. S. A. , 1976. 48p.) Gr. 3-10.

Charming illustrations that will appeal to all readers complement the author's thoughts about love. Love is viewed as a wonderful feeling that conquers, beautifies, discovers, guards, finds, exists, and conduces to all the beautiful things. I wonder how many young readers will be so enthralled by "love. "

m   Medina Mora, Mónica. Las desventuras del sol. (México: Litográfica Turmex, 1976. 14p.) Gr. 1-3.

Bold illustrations, pleasing presentation and long, "preachy" text describe the sad adventures of the sun as he envied the importance of water. Only by ignoring the moralistic text which emphasizes that "todos tenemos algo que dar" [we all have something to give], children will enjoy the bright, gay illustrations.

m Nervo, Amado. Lecturas literarias. (México: Editorial
   Patria, 1972. 312p.) Gr. 9-12.

   Anthology of selections of Mexican, Latin American
   and Spanish classics which show the gracefulness of the
   Spanish language. Some of the authors represented are
   Cervantes, Calderón de la Barca, Gutiérrez Nájera,
   Ruben Darío, Benito Juárez and Lope de Vega.

nr Ponce Sánchez, Angela. Cuentos para mis nietos.
   (México: Editorial Alvarez y Alvarez, 1972. 77p.)
   Gr. 6-9.

   Collection of ten moralistic stories written by a
   loving grandmother to her grandchildren "as proof of her
   mature and delicate love. " Unfortunately the righteous
   actions of her characters are neither interesting nor
   touching. The cheap paper also does not add to its
   homely presentation.

nr Robles, Antonio. Historia de Azulita y Rompetacones.
   (México: Secretaría de Educación Pública, 1968. 510p.)
   Gr. 2-4.

   Long, dull, narrations and descriptions and the
   author's insistence in "cleaning" all fairy tales of mor-
   bidities have resulted in stories for children that lack
   interest and action.

nr _____. Rompetacones y 100 cuentos más. (México:
   Secretaría de Educación Pública, 1962. 520p.) Gr.
   2-4.

   This is a collection of sixty spiritless and tedious
   traditional fairy tales that have been carefully "cleaned"
   by the author of all violence and vengeance. The author
   emphasizes that the true mission of literature for children should be goodness and that all children should
   learn to forgive.

m Salinas, Miguel, editor. Cuentos, leyendas y poemas.
   (México: Imprenta Aldina, 1975. 258p.) Gr. 9-12.

   This is a collection of nineteenth-century stories,
   legends and poems of Mexican, Spanish, Argentinean,
   Venezuelan and Nicaraguan authors. The intent is to
   educate students about geography, history, mythology,

vocabulary and the ability to express themselves correctly through the writings of Rafael Delgado, Ruben Darío, Amado Nervo, Manuel Gutiérrez Nájera and others.

nr   Serrano, Amparo Espinosa de.   Hola Jesús.   (México: n. p. , n. d.   36p.)   Gr. 1-3.

Graceless illustrations and stale text describe what are supposedly children's feelings about their families, nature, death, Mexico's problems, and God.   It emphasizes faith and the goodness of God.

*   Serrano Martínez, Celedonio.   El cazador y sus perros. (México: Luis Fernandez, 1959.   135p.)   Gr. 9-12.

Hunting novel which describes the author's feelings for the Mexican countryside.   It is written as a collection of short poetic stories about flowers, the seasons, darkness, rain, illusions and remembrances.

HISTORY

m   La conquista de Mexico.   (Barcelona: Editorial Teide, n. d.   78p.)   Gr. 9-12.

This is the conquest of Mexico as told by the Spaniards with colorful illustrations.   The lengthy descriptions and long text (78 pages) make it supplementary reading for older high-school students.   It emphasizes the Spaniards' desire to evangelize in the New World and to "abolir para siempre sus [the Indians] ritos exóticos" (p. 9).   It describes Cortés as a strong and dedicated man and justifies him as a man of his time using violence to Christianize the Indians.   This book does not describe the achievements of the pre-Columbian Indians but it is a useful book in showing the Spaniards' version of the Conquest, such as an incident in which "Cortés trató de hablar con el emperador Azteca, pero si bien este le fijó en diversas ocasiones una entrevista, no acudió nunca a ella.   Entonces el terrible avance continuó" (p. 70).

*   Consejos de un padre a su hija.   Traducción de Miguel León-Portilla.   (México: Instituto Nacional Protección Infancia, 1974.   28p.)   Gr. 1-12.

Beautiful illustrations of a pre-Columbian father's
advice to his daughter. It expresses the father's love
for his daughter, it cautions her about life's problems
and sufferings, it describes the pleasant things of life
and naturally accepts the need for sex education: "y
finalmente el acto sexual, por el cual se hace siembra
de gente." And ends: "He cumplido mi oficio, mucha-
chita mía, niñita mía. Que seas feliz, que Nuestro
Señor te haga dichosa."

* Díaz del Castillo, Bernal. Verdadera historia de los
sucesos de la conquista de la nueva España. Adaptación
por Luis Hernandez Alfonso. Illus: Eduardo Santonja.
(Madrid: Aguilar, 1965. 110p.) Gr. 10-adult.

Outstanding adaptation of the classic work that describes the conquest of Mexico written in 1568 by Bernal
Díaz del Castillo who accompanied Cortés in his expedi-
tions to the New World, 1519-1527. Important episodes
in the conquest of Mexico are interestingly described and
vividly illustrated in this fast-moving narrative. The
reader is exposed to the famous Indian, Doña Marina,
Cortés' translator and companion (p. 11); to human sacrifice as practiced by pre-Columbian Indians (p. 15); to
the marvelous variety and richness of Aztec market-
places (p. 27); to the unfortunate murder of Montezuma
(p. 42); and to the many battles and jealousies that surrounded the conquest of Mexico.

* León-Portilla, Miguel. La familia Náhuatl prehispánica.
Illus: Raúl Guerra Meléndez. (México: Instituto
Nacional Protección Infancia, 1975. 134p.) Gr. 10-
adult.

Excellent description of pre-Columbian Nahuatl family
life with attractive pre-Columbian illustrations in color.
Unfortunately the cheap paper and magazine format detract from its value. It describes the importance of the
family to pre-Columbian people, the strict sex laws
(adultery was punishable by death), the existence of pros-
titution, the education of young people in the seriousness
of marriage, the use of birth control, and the importance
of children in the family. Because of the vocabulary and
subject matter it is highly recommended for mature high
school students.

LEGENDS

* González Casanova, Pablo. <u>Cuentos indígenas.</u> (México:
Universidad Nacional Autónoma de Mexico, 1965. 160p.)
Gr. 5-12.

     Excellent collection of short pre-Columbian legends
of animals. It includes on one side of the page the
Nahuatl version and on the other side the author's Spanish translation.

* Mischne, Bella, and Carmen Vidal. <u>Cuentos mexicanos.</u>
Illus: Vilarchao y Perellón. (Madrid: Doncel, 1966.
32p.) Gr. 2-9.

     Two pre-Columbian legends. The first, "El
inocente pájaro pujuy," is a Mayan legend which tells of
the naive, innocent, shy bird "Pujuy" which lost all its
beautiful, elegant feathers to the ambition and variety of
the peacock. The "pujuy" is still waiting for the peacock
to return to him all its colorful feathers. The second,
"El mensaje de Quetzalcoatl," is an Aztec legend which
tells of the marvels of Tenochtitlán: its exquisite gar-
dens, fascinating canals, marvelous jewels in gold, sil-
ver, precious stones and textiles. It also describes the
courage of their leaders, the importance of human sacrifice to their God Huitzilopochtli, the arrival of the Spanish conquerors with their belief in one God and the author's added moral judgment of the Aztecs' sacrifice
"por ignorancia y barbarie se había derramado tanta
sangre inocente, en lo más alto del templo, se alzó la
cruz" (p. 32).

* Saldaña de Gibbons, Angelina. <u>Tejocote--cuentos de la
sierra mexicana.</u> (México: Novaro, 1971. 85p.) Gr.
9-12.

     Well-known Mexican tales but some unfortunately are
too complicated and too long for young readers. The
better selections, which include more action and shorter
descriptions, are "La burrita encantada," "Los tres
consejos," and "La apuesta." Colorful illustrations add
interest to the tales.

PERU

BIOGRAPHY

* Howard, Cecil. <u>Pizarro y la conquista del Perú.</u>
(Barcelona: Editorial Timun Mas, 1971. 98p.) Gr.
9-12.

The conquest of Peru and Pizarro's role as the
conqueror is fascinatingly portrayed in this attractive
book with interesting descriptions and beautiful color
photographs dispersed throughout. Spain's role in the
conquest, the outstanding achievements of the Inca
Empire, the jealousies, quarrels, and murders of the
Spanish Conquistadores, all are explained. Some interesting facts about the Incan Empire are: "Todo el
imperio estaba unido por una red de carreteras que
hubieran podido rivalizar con las construidas por los
romanos ... tenía ancho de unos 7.5 metros" (p. 36).
"Si la civilización inca tenía un fallo importante, era el
no haber sabido desarrollar un sistema de escritura"
(p. 38). "Sistemas de canales y acueductos que
revelaban un buen concimiento de la ingeniería, habían
convertido las zonas áridas en vergeles" (pp. 53-54).
And about Pizarro: "Su aspecto le favorecía y cuando
estaba profundamente emocionado hablaba muy bien.
Pero él también era un hombre de cuna humilde,
analfabeto, que había pasado su vido con toscos caballeros, y no tenía modales de caballero" (p. 58).

FICTION

nr Barrionuevo, Alfonsina. <u>La chica de la cruz.</u> (Perú:
n.p., 1976. 111p.) Gr. 9-12.

One year in the life of a ten-year-old girl, Caro,
who experiences humiliations and undue punishments
from her unkind Aunt Mercedes. Long descriptions of

the most complicated religious penalties that trouble Caro
make this story difficult to read or enjoy. It includes a
few good insights into the life of the very rich and the
very poor in Peru, and the separation of the "whites"
and the "Indians," but the story is an obscure tale of
religious censures.

m _____. Pintadita la vikuña. Illus: Kukuli Velarde
Barrionuevo. (Perú: Editorial Arica, n.d.   61p.)   Gr.
4-8.

Through the story of Pituka, a nine-year-old girl,
and Pintadita, a new-born vicuña, we are introduced to
the life of vicuñas in Peru.   It includes many Quechua
words as it describes Pituka's feelings and thoughts
against the shooting of vicuñas to capture their expensive
wool.   This is a moving story about a Quechua Indian
(Inca) girl, and her adorable vicuña which might interest
readers with a good knowledge of the Spanish language.

nr Cerna Guardia, Rosa. Los días de Carbón. (Perú:
Sección Peruana de la Organización Internacional del
Libro Juvenil, 1966.   88p.)   Gr. 7-12.

As stated in the prologue of this Peruvian award-
winning book, children's literature should offer children
"a message of beauty and edifying feelings for a better
Humanity" (p. 9).   The author expressed many commend-
able beliefs in this story about a dog, Carbón, and its
relationship with nature, men and children, but its long
descriptions and tedious admonitions certainly do not
make it enjoyable reading.

nr _____. El hombre de paja. (Perú: Editorial
Universo, 1972.   126p.)   Gr. 3-6.

This is an award-winning collection of Peruvian
stories that, however, cannot possibly be enjoyed by
children.   As stated by Carlota Carvallo de Nuñez in
the prologue, the author writes literature "to awaken in
children feelings of solidarity, understanding and toler-
ance among men."   Unfortunately this results in a wearisome text that abounds in pedantic, moralistic insinua-
tions, such as, "ahora, pajarito, sólo falta que te
enciendas, que irradies, que pongas tu alma ..." (p.
23) and "No, no es por el interés de las cosas pequeñas
que me muevo aquí.   Es por amor a la niñez, y el amor

no vive de mezquindades, sino de una entrega total y
absoluta" (p. 104).   Only the simple, two-tone illustrations will attract young readers.

*   Cremer, Gabriela. <u>Las aventuras de Chalaquito.</u> (Perú:
     Editorial Universo, 1969.   30p.)   Gr. K-2.

     Attractive story about a Peruvian blue bus that
travels every day from the city of Lima to the port in
Callao.   Bold illustrations depict Chalaquito's adventures
through Peruvian mountains and towns.   It shows glimpses
of the people and llamas of Peru.   Simple vocabulary,
charming story and splendid illustrations make this one
of the best picture books from Latin America.

nr   Díaz Herrera, Jorge. <u>Parque de leyendas.</u>   (Perú:
     Instituto de Cultura, 1977.   75p.)   Gr. 6-9.

     Collection of seventeen morose stories and poems in
which the author "rebels against the traditional literature
for children and describes the reality of life, so that
the child may build upon it the wonderful world of his
imagination. "   Using a combination of rhyme and prose,
the author describes the life of lonely flowers, abandoned
animals, desolate fishermen, and other miseries.   How
sad to believe that life is only a collection of adversities.

nr   Eguren, Mercedes, and José Hidalgo. <u>El muñeco de</u>
     <u>Aserrín y otros cuentos.</u>   <u>Muñeca de Trapo.</u>   Illus:
     Charo Núñez de Patrucco.   (Perú: Premio Juan Volatín,
     1969.   119p.)   Gr. 3-6.

     Even though these two authors won the Juan Volatin
children's literature award, because of M. Eguren's
"charming, simple and tender stories" and J. Hidalgo's
"valuable and delicate poetic prose, " I do not believe
that these stories can be enjoyed by children of any age.
Their complex themes with sophisticated educational or
moralistic messages are unappealing and tedious.
Hidalgo's vocabulary is too pretentious and his messages
unbelievably pathetic.   Only the simple, two-tone illustrations are directed to the enjoyment of children.

m   Gonzalez, Francisco. <u>Vida de perros.</u> Illus: Enrique
     Zegarra Torres. (Perú: Ediciones Fragor, 1977.   34p.)
     Gr. 4-8.

Collection of four short stories that describe the "real life of some dogs" that the author knew. The author pretends to show dogs as symbols of fidelity. Dog lovers might have mixed feelings when reading about mistreated and abused dogs that die alone and forgotten.

m   Izquierdo Ríos, Francisco. El colibrí con cola de pavo real. (Perú: Talleres Gráficos Villanuevo, 1965. 57p.) Gr. 3-6.

These are four nature stories that describe different geographical areas of Peru written in a monotonous style. The stories center around the forests, mountains, jungles and rivers as well as the animals of Peru. Eight two-tone illustrations may add to their appeal, but the stories are uninspired and not easy to enjoy.

m   _____. La literatura infantil en el Perú. (Perú: Casa de la Cultura, 1969. 90p.) Gr. adult.

Brief essay which describes the author's beliefs regarding "good" and "bad" children's literature. The author regrets the lack of children's literature in Peru showing its diversified geography. He expresses extreme concern in allowing children to read certain books, such as Las mil y una noches (Thousand and One Nights) and Bocaccio's El decamerón (The Decameron) because these books may cause children "immense damage" and "this self-inflicted damage would be huge and irreparable" (p. 14). He condemns Thousand and One Nights because "it may represent a destructive influence in children's personalities because of its overflowing fantasy and the sensuality that it contains" (p. 13). The author is a great admirer of Walt Disney's "creative genius, " and he disapproves of most of Peru's children's literature because of its excessive didactisism and "intentions to instruct" (p. 19). The second part of the book is an anthology which includes a collection of complicated poems and tolerable stories by Peruvian authors.

m   Nuñez, Carlota Carvallo de. Cuentos de Navidad. Illus: Charo Nuñez de Patrucco. (Perú: Ediciones Peisa, n. d. 93p.) Gr. 9-12.

This is a collection of ten fantasy stories that describe the lifestyles of upper middle-class children and

the miseries of the very poor children in Peru in a combination of strange happenings, such as religious miracles and dead people helping unfortunate children. Nine
attractive and colorful illustrations add a much needed
lightness to the stories.

*   Olave, María del Pilar. La gallinita costurera y otros
cuentos. (Perú: Editorial Arica, n. d. 28p.) Gr. 1-3.

Attractive collection of eight well-known animal
stories with small, pretty illustrations: "La gallinita
costurera," "Los tres chanchitos," "Medio pollito," "El
osito miedoso," "El gallo de boda," "El corderito blanco,"
"Los tres erizos," "El gato con bota." The themes and
simple vocabulary make this collection a delight for
young readers.

m   . Las pintas de las mariquitas y otros cuentos.
(Perú: Editorial Arica, n. d. 28p.) Gr. 2-5.

Collection of seven animal stories and one story
about a magic pot. The vocabulary might be appropriate
for better readers. The small illustrations in color do
not lend themselves to storytelling. The titles are "Las
Pintas de las Mariquitas," "La llamita generosa," "El
ratoncito roequeso," "Las tres piedrecitas mágicas,"
"La ollita mágica," "La lechucita que no podía dormir,"
"Pollito Tito," and "La guerra de los higos."

nr Roggero, Cecilia de. Garabatos. Illus: Constanza
Pérez Rosas. (Perú: Editorial Arica, n. d. 92p.)
Gr. 3-6.

Wearisome collection of thirty stories that remind
one of dull essays in which the author expresses her
opinions about life, death, dreams, and whatever comes
to her mind. Only the illustrations might appeal to
children; the text is a certain bore.

nr Vega Herrera, César. La noche de los sprunkos.
(Perú: Imprenta Editorial El Sol, 1974. 164p.) Gr.
6-8.

Long, dull collection of adventures that through
exemplary lessons in "good" behavior pretend to entertain children. "Sprunkos" are the most charming, good
and happy beings in all the world, and through them,

the reader is exposed to history lessons, proper manners, adequate care of animals, etc. This tedious book
won the National Children's Literature Award in 1969 in
Peru.

nr   _____. Pasakón. (Perú: n. p. , 1976? 24p.) Gr.
   3-6.

The author lectures on peace, injustice, misery,
and poverty and summarizes his concern about the state
of the world by asserting that "children are not to be
blamed because this world is made only for business and
for the pleasures of those that have money." The depressing, complicated thoughts expressed by the author,
the long descriptions, and the simple illustrations result
in one man's view of the world, but to think that this
book is intended for children is beyond my imagination.

HISTORY

m Baeza, José. El imperio de los Incas. (Barcelona:
Ediciones Araluce, 1973. 160p.) Gr. 9-12.

Historical narrative of pre-Columbian Peru written
for young adults in 160 pages. It includes eight short
illustrations depicting Inca life. The vocabulary and
lack of attractive illustrations make this book recommended only to the unusual student. Some samples of
the interesting descriptions are: "También allí existía
una religión que se anteponía a todos los deberes,
tambíen allí había reyes, y grandes edificios de piedra,
y soberbios templos y magníficos caminos. En cambio,
eran analfabetos, no tenían más medio de navegación que
las balsas, ni más vehículos terrestres que las sillas
de mano.... Su cerámica y sus tejidos fueron la
admiración de los españoles" (p. 7). And describing
Incan palaces: "estaban tan bien cuidados como si
pasara en ellos la vida y tenían los mismos lujos y
comodidades que la residencia imperial de Cuzco" (p.
122-123). It describes Huaina Capac the great Inca who
established the large empire, Huascar his eldest son,
and Atahualpa who later usurped the throne and was the
last Inca chief.

LEGENDS

* Alegría, Ciro. <u>Panki y el guerrero.</u> (Perú: Industrial
Gráfica, 1968. 95p.) Gr. 6-12.

   Collection of sixteen legends from the Amazon region, the Peruvian Andes, Chile, Brazil, Mexico, and
Colombia which narrate supernatural beliefs and popular
tales. They are written in a fast-moving pace and have
striking illustrations. Several of the shorter legends,
such as "De cómo repartió el diablo los males por el
mundo" (p. 34), and "Leyenda del Ayaymama" (p. 18)
may be enjoyed by all readers. These legends have
maintained their original pre-Columbian and popular
flavor.

m Barrionuevo, Alfonsina. <u>El Muki y otros personajes</u>
<u>fabulosos.</u> (Perú: n. p., 1974. 33p.) Gr. 9-12. In
Spanish and English.

   The varied and fantastic mythology of Peru is described in a complex style full of old myths, gods,
nightmares, magic characters and an unreal world. The
attractive, colorful illustrations add a much needed
lightness to the confusing descriptions of moral rules,
treacherous gods, sinful priests, etc. The English text
is easier to read and may appeal to those students who
will find the Spanish text too confusing.

* Jordana Laguna, José Luis. <u>Leyendas amazónicas.</u>
(Madrid: Doncel, 1976. 138p.) Gr. 3-10.

   Excellent collection of twenty-one Peruvian legends
of the Amazon region written in a most delightful, natural style. In brief, spontaneous narratives they explain
why it rains on the earth, the origin of the sun and the
moon, children's proper behavior, why the sun shines
every day, birds' happiness, early man's cooking habits,
the origin of the Amazon River, and many other important aspects of life in the Amazon jungle. Colorful illustrations complement each legend.

* Palma, Ricardo. <u>Tradiciones peruanas.</u> (Madrid:
Aguilar, 1962. 98p.) Gr. 9-12.

   Brief essays with small, simple illustrations of life
during Inca times, the Conquest, Colonial and modern

Peru. Outstanding witty examples are "Los tres motivos del oidor" (1544) p. 9, "Juez y enamoradizo (1630), "Creo que hay infierno" (1790) p. 47. The variety of themes make this an appealing introduction to Peru.

* Soler Blanch, Carmen. <u>Leyendas incas.</u> (Barcelona: Instituto de Artes Gráficas, 1964. 194p.) Gr. 9-12.

Outstanding collection of forty-six legends showing the rich oral tradition which belonged to the pre-Columbian Incas and which was written down by the Spaniards. Of special interest are the following legends that tell about the great Inca leaders and the Spanish conquerors: "Los dos enemigos" (p. 37-39) shows two warriors from Atahualpa's army that hated each other and their sad ending; "Viracocha y el príncipe" (p. 41-45) demonstrates the high values held by the Incas; "Funesto presagio" (p. 47-49) tells about Cori Duchicela, Atahualpa's wife and her "doleful premonition. " "El augurio" (p. 61-63) describes the sad ending of Huaina Capac's reign as a result of the Spaniards' arrival; "Las lágrimas del peñón" (p. 75-76) tells how the Spaniards only wanted to take gold from the Incas; "La jugada de ajedrez" (p. 135-136) tells about Atahualpa's chess game and how he learned to play, with tragic results; "La flor de la Laguna Urcus" (p. 157-158) describes the mortal envy of the two brothers Huáscar and Atahualpa.

* Sologuren, Javier, editor. <u>Cuentos y leyendas infantiles.</u> (Perú: Casa de la Cultura del Peru, 1970. 152p.) Gr. 6-12.

Outstanding collection of well-known fairy tales, legends and stories from countries around the world written in a simple, easy-to-understand language. It includes legends from Asia, Europe and Russia, classical fairy tales and stories and legends by Peruvian authors, such as Ricardo Palma, Carlota Carvallo de Núñez and Francisco Izquierdo Ríos. Unfortunately the unattractive presentation of this book (cheap paper, no illustrations) might not appeal to young readers, but the brief and simple stories could certainly be used to read aloud to students.

POETRY

* Olave, María del Pilar. <u>Poesía menuda.</u> (Perú:

Editorial Arica, 1972.   28p.)   Gr. 1-3.

Attractive collection of rhymes and poems with simple, colorful illustrations of themes well-known to children: parents and home, games and toys, animals, nature and Christmas.

PUERTO RICO

FICTION

nr   Benet, Evelyn Méndez de. <u>Cuentos y risas.</u> (Puerto
Rico: Departamento de Instrucción Pública, 1971. 80p.)
Gr. 2-4.

Collection of mediocre stories, rhymes and riddles
with illustrations that will not attract young readers.
Some of the selections could be used as reading exercises, such as "Alfabeto cómico" (p. 75), "La fiesta de
las letras" (p. 79), and "Para soltar la lengua solamente"
(p. 66).

nr   Diaz Montero, Aníbal. <u>Pedruquito y sus amigos.</u>
(Spain: M. Pareja, 1967. 130p.) Gr. 3-6.

Collection of thirty-five brief animal stories which
show Pedruquito in the forest with his favorite dog.
The unattractive presentation; minuscule, uninspired
black-and-white illustrations, and repetitive animal adventures make this book unappealing to young readers.

*   Laguerre, Enrique A. , editor. <u>Antología de cuentos
puertorriqueños.</u> (México: Editorial Orión, 1975.
175p.) Gr. 9-adult.

Outstanding collection of twenty brief Puerto Rican
short stories that are entertaining and enjoyable to read.
They include a few popular Puerto Rican legends, and
short stories about love, marriage, mystery and various
other human situations written by fifteen well-known
Puerto Rican authors. The simple writing style and the
interesting and varied themes will delight most readers.

*   _____. <u>La llamarada.</u> (Puerto Rico: Editorial
Cultural, 1975. 234p.) Gr. 10-adult.

Proclaimed by many as "the great Puerto Rican
novel," this work, originally published in 1935, will be
enjoyed by sophisticated readers interested in psycholog-
ical novels that emphasize social problems. Through
the thoughts and feelings of the main character, the
reader is exposed to the injustices that occur at the
sugarcane plantations. The traditions and the daily life
of the Puerto Rican plantation owners as well as the
jíbaros (peasants) are poignantly described.

* Mendez Ballester, Manuel. Isla Cerrera. (Spain: M.
Pareja, 1941. 285p.) Gr. 10-adult.

Outstanding historical novel that describes in fascinating detail the early years of Spanish Colonial life in
Puerto Rico. Through the adventurous life of Ricardo
de Boadilla, the reader is exposed to dangerous sea
journeys, terrifying slave ships, frequent Indian upris-
ings, complicated love affairs, and the hard labor of
colonizing a new hacienda. The marvelous human dilem-
mas of the main character, as well as the exciting adventures in this novel, will entice any reader with a good
knowledge of Spanish.

m Muckley, Robert L., editor. Cuentos puertorriqueños.
(Illinois: National Textbook Co. 1974. 85p.) Gr. 9-
adult.

Nine short stories written by Puerto Rican authors
for Spanish-speakers in which they want "to show the
genuine feelings of their people." These stories are
directed towards students whose native tongue is Spanish. Several of the stories discuss political issues such
as, "Una caja de plomo que ho se podía abrir," which
is a strong protest against militarism; "Oh, sey can yu
sí bai de don-serly lai ..." describes the feelings of a
Puerto Rican teacher from New York as he debates
whether to have Puerto Rican children in Puerto Rico
sing the United States national anthem. The complex
themes and difficult vocabulary make these stories better
suited for adults or dedicated Puerto Rican students.

m Nieves Falcón, Luis. Poemas y colores. Illus: Rafael
Rivera Rosa. (Puerto Rico: Editorial Edil, 1968. 28p.)
Gr. K-2.

Young children's paintings illustrate simple animals,

flowers, and dogs with a Puerto Rican background. The uninspired text and unsophisticated children's illustrations make this a mediocre picture book.

m   Rosario, Rubén del. A B C de Puerto Rico. (Connecticut: Troutman Press, 1968. 54p.) Gr. 1-3.

Striking two-tone illustrations are the background of this cultural abecedarium with Puerto Rican content. Even though it is written for primary readers, I am afraid that the abstract poems and difficult vocabulary that exemplify each word make it impossible for children to enjoy or understand.

m   Troutman Plenn, Doris. La canción verde. Illus: Paul Galdone. (Connecticut: The Troutman Press, 1956. 102p.) Gr. 4-8.

Fantasy story about a Puerto Rican cricket who travels to New York City. The cricket lived enchantedly in his island of eternal spring, as he had never heard of other places. The cricket's adventures on the plane and in the big city are described as well as his delighted return to his island. And his message: "Diré a todos que el mundo es bello y tiene perfecta unidad ... " (I will tell everybody that the world is beautiful and that it has perfect unity).

m   Zeno Gandia, Manuel. La charca. (Puerto Rico: Instituto de Cultura Puertorriqueña, 1975. 266p.) Gr. 10-adult.

Lond, detailed novel written in 1894 by an eminent Puerto Rican author, politician and scientist. The varied characters and their tragic lives depict scenes of passion, murder, avarice and constant misfortune. This novel might interest readers with a good knowledge of Spanish who enjoy lots of action as well as long philosophical discussions about life, religion and patriotism.

LEGENDS

*   Alegría, Ricardo E. Cuentos folklóricos de Puerto Rico. Illus: Rafael Seco. (Puerto Rico: Colección de Estudios Puertorriqueños, 1974. 120p.) Gr. 3-6.

Twelve well-known Puerto Rican folktales written in
simple language but unfortunately the illustrations are
disfigured and blurred.   Some outstanding titles are:
"Los tres hermanos y los objectos maravillosos" (p. 11),
"Juan Bobo y la Princesa Adivinadora" (p. 31), "Juan
Bobo, la puerca, los pollos y el caldero" (p. 69), "Los
tres deseos" (p. 25).   The simple fluid writing style of
these tales makes them truly enjoyable reading.

* Belpré, Pura. Oté. Illus: Paul Galdone. (New York:
   Pantheon Books, 1969. 28p.) Gr. 1-3.

Puerto Rican folktale narrated by the well-known
Puerto Rican librarian Pura Belpré, as she remembers
it told by her grandfather.   The tale describes a very
poor family who did not have enough to eat.   The father,
Oté, found the near-sighted devil who ended up eating
most of the family's food.   Oté would not follow the
advice of the old woman and the family had to be saved
by Chiquitin's courage.

* _____. Pérez y Martina. Illus: Carlos Sánchez M.
   (New York: Warne, 1961. 58p.) Gr. 1-3.

Entertaining version of the popular Puerto Rican
folktale, Pérez y Martina, with attractive colorful illustrations written in simple language.   The repetitive
marriage proposals by diverse animals to the attractive
and royal Spanish cockroach maiden will amuse children
as well as the surprising ending in which the elegant
mouse Perez, falls to his death into a boiling bottle.

* Coll y Toste, Cayetano Dr.   Leyendas puertorriqueñas.
   (México: Editorial Orión, 1974. 202p.) Gr. 9-12.

Puerto Rican author of the late 1800's that intended
(and succeeded) in writing simple, and in direct language,
the legends of Puerto Rico.   The format is, unfortunately, unattractive: paper, typesetting, etc. , but his approach to the history of his country is enjoyable as well
as informative.   It includes four legends of the sixteenth
century, three of the seventeenth century, three of the
eighteenth century, and two of the nineteenth century.
The historical notes at the end of each legend further
explain the content of the legends.   Very good reading
for seriously interested students of Puerto Rico.

HISTORY

* Alegría, Ricardo E. Descubrimiento, conquista y
colonización de Puerto Rico. (Spain: Colección de
Estudios Puertorriqueños, 1971. 175p.) Gr. 6-12.

Excellent introduction to the discovery, conquest and
colonization of Puerto Rico written in simple, easy-to-
understand text. It also includes outstanding color and
black-and-white reproductions of paintings, maps and
drawings that greatly enhance the readers' interest of
the fifteenth and sixteenth centuries of life in Puerto
Rico and Europe.

m   . Historia de Nuestros Indios, versión elemen-
tal. (Spain: Manuel Pareja, 1974. 84p.) Gr. 2-4.

In simple text and easy-to-read explanations, the
reader is introduced to the history of the Indians of
Puerto Rico. It includes the discovery of the Indians,
their origins, furniture, housing, family, dress, govern-
ment, religion, fishing, hunting, transportation, games,
war and heritage. Unfortunately the insipid two-tone
illustrations do not add much interest to the historical
narrative.

NON-FICTION

* Nieves Falcón, Luis. Mi música. Illus: Rafael
Rivera Rosa. (Puerto Rico: Editorial Edil, 1975.
25p.) Gr. 3-6.

Bold, colorful illustrations and easy-to-understand
descriptions tell about the musical instruments, dances,
songs, and music of Puerto Rico. The historical background as well as interesting information make this a
valuable and enjoyable book.

m Ribes Tobar, Federico. Puerto Rico en mi corazón.
Illus: Izzy Sanabria. (New York: Plus Ultra Educational Publishers, 1972. 32p.) Gr. 3-6.

Mediocre illustrations with interesting text in Spanish and English describe basic information about Puerto
Rico, such as, discovery and colonization, origins,
privateers and pirates, heroes, the jíbaro, music and

dancing, animals, etc. This book is well written, with notable facts about Puerto Rico.

THEATER

m   Marquis, René.   La carreta.   (Puerto Rico: Editorial
    Cultural, 1963.   172p.)   Gr.   10-adult.

    Considered by many critics as one of the best social dramas written by a Puerto Rican author, this play dramatizes the life of a poor peasant family that moves to New York City in search of a better life, but in two years returns to Puerto Rico to rebuild their anguished lives. The use of Puerto Rican pronunciation of the Spanish language makes the reading of this play a difficult task. Letters have been removed or substituted throughout the dialogues to authenticate Puerto Rican dialect.

nr Palma, Marigloria.   Teatro para niños.   (Spain:
    Ediciones Rumbos, 1968.   153p.)   Gr. 6-8.

    Collection of seven uninspired plays for children about animals and fruits that are intended to amuse children. But the complicated vocabulary, obscure verses, and dull themes will not encourage children to read or to act these plays.

SPAIN

BIOGRAPHY

* Alavedra, José. La extraordinaria vida de Pablo Casals. (Barcelona: Aymá, 1969. 121p.) Gr. 6-12.

The artistic development of this great Spanish cellist is exquisitely portrayed by the author, who knew Casals very well. It describes Casals' youth, his musical education in Barcelona, Madrid and Paris, and his successes as a master cellist and composer. Very little mention is made of Casals' wife, Martita.

m Blázquez, Feliciano. Juan XXIII. (Madrid: Editorial Hernando, 1976. 160p.) Gr. 9-12.

Pope John XXIII was born into a poor family in Italy in 1881. This biography describes his early years as Angelo Roncalli, his experiences during World War II, and his life as Pope John. This book includes biographical narration about Pope John's life and supplementary historical information that further elaborates on important facts of the times.

* Flores de Lemus, Isabel. Cervantes. (Barcelona: Vilamala, 1970. 225p.) Gr. 7-12.

This is an outstanding biography of Cervantes. It is a marvelous introduction to the great author, his times and his works. It describes important facts of Cervantes' life, the courts of Carlos V and Felipe II, and the power of the Catholic Church. It includes samples of Cervantes' poetry, philosophy and essays.

m Martínez Laínez, Fernando. Miguel Servet. (Madrid: Editorial Hernando, 1976. 160p.) Gr. 9-12.

Detailed biography of Miguel Servet, born in 1511,

68

who lived a most controversial life with the religious
powers of his time.   It describes the intolerance of the
Spanish Inquisition in Spain, Servet's achievements in
medicine, and, finally, Servet's unfortunate challenge of
John Calvin's ideas, which caused Servet's death. This
book includes biographical narration about Servet's life
and supplementary historical information that further
elaborates on important facts of the times.

m   Molina Llorente, María Pilar.   El terrible florentino.
    (Madrid: Doncel, 1973.   102p.)   Gr. 7-12.

      This is an interesting biography with gorgeous illus-
trations of Michelangelo's finest works.   It is written in
a very vivid style, but, unfortunately, the author emphasizes a strong religious message.   The greatness of
Michelangelo's works and talent are beautifully portrayed.

*   Monleón, José.   García Lorca: vida y obra de un poeta.
    (Madrid: Aymá, 1974.   107p.)   Gr. 10-adult.

      This is an excellent introduction to García Lorca's
thought and works.   Part I describes the year 1898, in
which García Lorca was born, and the defeat of Spain
by the United States and its effect on the leadership of
Spain in the world.   The book analyzes García Lorca's
plays, puppet shows and poetry and, amazingly for books
published in Spain, hints at the loss of great Spanish
thinkers in their civil war in the 1930's.   It shows
García Lorca's interest in gypsies, bullfighters, and
New York City.   García Lorca was killed by the new
Regime in Spain in 1936--it surprised me to read this
fact in this book.

m   Montero, Isaac.   Abraham Lincoln.   (Madrid: Editorial
    Hernando, 1976.   162p.)   Gr. 9-12.

      Well-written biography of Abraham Lincoln that be-
gins with Lincoln's murder and includes important aspects of his personal and political life.   The outstanding
presentation of this book (appropriate black-and-white
photographs of Lincoln's life and times, well-placed subject headings, attractive type and format) as well as
supplementary historical information that further elaborates on important issues of the times, make this a
recommended biography in Spanish of the great American president.

*   Palau y Fabré, José. La extraordinaria vida de Picasso.
(Barcelona: Aymá, 1972. 100p.) Gr. 7-12.

This is an outstanding biography which explains
Picasso's artistic development through the use of excel-
lent photographs of his greatest works. It comments on
Picasso's different styles and art forms.

nr   Tudela, Mariano. Vida del joven Andersen. (Madrid:
Doncel, 1963. 153p.) Gr. 8-10.

This biography describes the early years of the
Danish author, but moralizes on the need for hard work
and perseverance through Andersen's difficult life. The
story-teller's sufferings and surroundings are appealingly
described.

CLASSICS

*   Cervantes Saavedra, Miguel de. Aventuras de Don
Quijote de la Mancha. Adaptación de Joaquín Aguirre
Bellver. Illus: C. Perellón. (Madrid: Edaf, 1972.
108p.) Gr. 5-12.

The enchanting dialogue and original humor of
Cervantes' Don Quijote has been maintained in this superb adaptation with beautiful illustrations of Don Quijote's
adventures.

*   Gefaell, María Luisa. El Cid. Illus: Laszlo Gal.
(Barcelona: Noguer, 1970. 135p.) Gr. 3-12.

The life and philosophy of the famous twelfth-century
Spanish knight, Don Rodrigo Díaz de Vivar, is magnificently illustrated in this handsome adaptation of the famous Spanish epic poem. There are splendid illustrations of Spanish feudal cities, kings and battles.

m   Jiménez, Juan Ramón. Platero y yo. Illus: Rafael
Munoa. (Madrid: Aguilar, 1972. 261p.) Gr. 7-12.

This book is required reading for all Spanish adolescents. Platero, a donkey, is the symbol of creation
with whom the author exchanges comments about nature.
The author wrote Platero "to narrate a historical, lyri-
cal anecdote of my youth. " It includes long, dull de-

scriptions of the house, food, and events of the author's
life.

* El Lazarillo de Tormes. Adapted by Basilio Losada.
Illus: C. Sanromâ. (Barcelona: Aftra Internacional,
1975. 166p.) Gr. 7-12.

This famous picaresque Spanish novel of the sixteenth
century with delightful illustrations has been magnificently
adapted for adolescents. It describes the adventures of
an orphan boy who, alone, must learn to survive in a
cruel and difficult world.

FICTION

nr Aguilê, Luis. Golito y un emisario de la cuarta
dimensiôn. Illus: Mariel Soria. (Barcelona: Editorial
Juventud, 1976. 43p.) Gr. 5-7.

Fantasy story that preaches to young readers about
the evilness of "material interests. " The author uses
long descriptions and interjects his personal teachings as
to the good life: "Dance is one of the purest expressions
of the spirit. " "Learn everything you can and would that
everything you learn be applied so that children of the
world will always be kind and pure. " "Innocence is the
perfect state of clean spirits. " Buried within these sermons is a magical story of two brothers and their magical triumphs over poverty.

* Amo, Montserrat del. Aparecen los "Blok. " Illus:
Rita Culla. (Barcelona: Juventud, 1971. 110p.) Gr.
3-6.

Zestful, humorous adventures in the lives of Spanish
children describe their relationships with their parents,
their friends, and their pets. Life in a Spanish suburb
is delightfully explored.

m _____. Los Blok y la bicicleta fantasma. (Barcelona:
Juventud, 1973. 123p.) Gr. 3-6.

This is an interesting mystery story of a missing
bicycle. Friendships are explored and a sick boy is
helped by the missing bicycle.

*   _____. Chitina y su gato. Illus: María Rius.
(Barcelona: Juventud, 1970. 14p.) Gr. K-2.

Splendid illustrations and simple, lively text combine
to make this story about Chitina and her cat a truly enjoyable animal story for young children.

nr   _____. La torre. Illus: Miguel Angel Pacheco.
(Valladolid: Editorial Miñón, 1975. 32p.) Gr. 4-6.

Luis is a young boy searching for his "tower of happiness. " He searches at a fair, but he cannot win; he builds
a kite, and he loses it; he manages to work at a petro-
leum camp, and the tower explodes; finally, he visits a
Spanish fortress built in the eleventh century and appar-
ently it is intact. But to Luis' utter dismay, the east
side of the tower is almost completely destroyed. Luis
is happy again when he realizes that he is the base of
his own happiness. Long descriptions and heavy philosophizing will not appeal to most young readers.

*   Benet, Amelia. David y los tulipanes. Illus: María
Rius. (Barcelona: Juventud, 1969. 14p.) Gr. K-2.

The happy life of middle-class Spanish children is
beautifully illustrated in this book that announces the arrival of spring. David and his sister Mireya are shown
going on a picnic and enjoying spring flowers, fruits and
birds.

m   _____. Miguel en invierno. Illus: María Rius.
(Barcelona: Juventud, 1970. 14p.) Gr. K-2.

Winter arrives with many new experiences for all
children. The illustrations show some typical Spanish
winter scenes: trees without leaves, cities without
lights, beaches without seashells, farmers at home, and
mothers preparing marmalade.

*   _____. Mireya en otoño. Illus: María Rius.
(Barcelona: Juventud, 1969. 15p.) Gr. K-2.

Beautiful color illustrations show Spanish children in
their various fall activities: visiting a vineyard and a
farm, sewing at home with mother, playing in a forest
and at school, and enjoying the rain.

*   . Silvia y Miguel en verano. Illus: Rosa Rius.
(Barcelona: Juventud, 1970. 14p.) Gr. K-2.

Attractive illustrations show Spanish children in their
summer activities: "Fiesta de San Juan," visits to the
countryside, school parties, parks, holiday preparations,
and trips to the beach.

nr Canela Garayoa, Mercê. ¿De quién es el bosque? Illus:
Montserrat Brucart. (Barcelona: La Galera, 1976.
99p.) Gr. 6-10.

Four boys and one girl (approximately ten to twelve
years old) are anxiously waiting for their summer holidays so that they may enjoy themselves playing in their
newly discovered oak tree. Their plans were almost
shattered when they learned that Don Jaime, the wealthy
landlord, was going to destroy all the oak trees and plow
the land for farming. The author elaborates on the dan-
gers of forest fires and the advantages of trees and forests to nature and humanity. The children in the story
are charming, but their adventures should have been
written in simpler language.

* Capdevila, Juan. Teo en avión. Illus: Violeta Denou.
(Barcelona: Editorial Timun Mas, 1977. 28p.) Gr.
1-3.

Teo describes his first airplane trip: the airport,
the pilot and copilot, a parachute, sleeping on the plane,
dreaming about Mars, eating on the plane, etc. Busy,
colorful illustrations complement the story.

*   . Teo en barco. Illus: Violeta Denou.
(Barcelona: Editorial Timun Mas, 1977. 28p.) Gr.
1-3.

Teo is playing at the beach and finds a message in-
viting him to go to visit an island. The ship is getting
ready to leave. Teo describes his experiences traveling
by ship as well as his arrival at the tropical island.
Colorful illustrations depict ship and ocean scenes.

*   . Teo en tren. Illus: Violeta Denou.
(Barcelona: Editorial Timun Mas, 1977. 28p.) Gr.
1-3.

Teo discovers an abandoned train engine. So, he

convinces his uncle, Luis, to take the whole family on a vacation. They go through the city, a gypsy camp, a pasture, a farm, over a river, inside a tunnel, and they finally arrive at the mountains to spend their vacation. Attractive, colorful illustrations depict train and nature scenes.

* Capmany, María Aurelia. Ni tuyo ni mío.... Illus: Carmen Solé. (Barcelona: La Galera, 1972. 22p.) Gr. 2-4.

Splendid, colorful illustrations describe a Spanish market in which adults are shown buying and selling vegetables, animals and clothes. Two boys who have nothing to sell and no money to buy agree that it must be dull spending your life buying and selling things.

* Carbo, Joaquín. La pandilla de los diez. Illus: Isidro Monés. (Barcelona: La Galera, 1969. 134p.) Gr. 3-6.

Firmly defined characters and original black-and-white illustrations tell the story of a gang of ten boys catching gangsters, roller skating and riding motorcycles. The unhappiness of one of the boys is understood by "the gang. "

m Castroviejo, Concepción. El jardín de las siete puertas. Illus: Fernando Benito. (Madrid: Doncel, 1968. 137p.) Gr. 3-6.

This is a collection of fourteen fantasy stories with handsome illustrations. Outstanding stories are "Tenemos las estrellas, " in which the themes of death, misery and happiness are explored; and "La tejedora de sueños" in which our need for dreams is described.

m Cervera, Juan. Los cuentos de Colorín. Illus: A. Perera A. Albarrán. (Spain: Ediciones Paulinas, 1976. 65p.) Gr. 3-5.

Collection of four stories with attractive illustrations that might appeal to good Spanish readers. The stories tell about lazy Monday that didn't want to work, a lonely butterfly that overcame her fears, selfish wheat grains that finally decided to grow, and a hungry dwarf that managed to live in a big house for a few days.

nr Cuadrench, Antonio. <u>La carta para mi amigo.</u> Illus:
    Pilarín Bayés. (Barcelona: La Galera, 1973. 24p.)
    Gr. K-2.

> Through a Spanish boy's penpal in Turkey, children
> are introduced to the mail service and mailmen. Unnec-
> essary educational exercises are included at the end of
> the story.

m   _____. <u>Erase una vez un pueblo....</u> Illus: Delbert
    Lederle. (Barcelona: La Galera, 1974. 20p.) Gr.
    K-2.

> A story that introduces children to city pollution
> through the growth of factories, automobiles and hotels.
> The sun stops shining, trees stop growing, and birds
> stop singing because nature and people have not been
> respected.

m   _____. <u>Los tres caballeros altos.</u> Illus: Pilarín
    Bayés. (Barcelona: La Galera, 1972. 18p.) Gr. K-2.

> Pleasing story of three tall gentlemen who are called
> by the king of a small European country to solve a seri-
> ous problem in his kingdom: all the people had become
> lazy and only wished to sleep. The three gentlemen
> humorously get all the townspeople back to work again.

*   Culla, Rita. <u>Rita en la cocina de su abuela.</u> (Barce-
    lona: Juventud, 1971. 16p.) Gr. K-2.

> Graceful illustrations show Rita in her grandmother's
> old-fashioned kitchen. She cannot understand why her
> mother "prefers a modern stove, plastic cupboards and
> counters, and water that comes from a faucet."

*   D'Atri, Adriana. <u>Así es nuestra casa.</u> Illus: Ulises
    Wensell. (Madrid: Ediciones Altea, 1977. 31p.) Gr.
    K-2.

> A seven-year-old girl and her six-year-old brother
> interestingly describe their house: the dining room that
> was converted into a much-needed bedroom, the hallway
> as an ideal place to play, the bedroom beds that mama
> said shouldn't be destroyed, the cluttered bathroom, and
> the many repairs that need to be done. The brief and
> simple text and the enchanting illustrations will delight

young children and also readers who are learning Spanish as a second language.

* _____. Así es nuestro hermano pequeño. Illus: Ulises Wensell. (Madrid: Ediciones Altea, 1977. 31p.) Gr. K-2.

A seven-year-old girl and her six-year-old brother charmingly tell us about their baby brother. They fondly describe various times and details in their lives from the moment that the baby was brought home from the hospital until he can walk on the beach holding mama's hand. The brief and simple text and the enchanting illustrations will delight young children and also readers who are learning Spanish as a second language.

* _____. Así es nuestro perro. Illus: Ulises Wensell. (Madrid: Ediciones Altea, 1977. 31p.) Gr. K-2.

A seven-year-old girl and her six-year-old brother describe their black dog, Carbón. Carbón arrived at their home when it was only two weeks old and the children recount many experiences with their dog: visits to friends' homes, fights with a parrot, learning to do tricks with their father, visits to the veterinarian, etc. The brief and simple text will delight young children and also readers who are learning Spanish as a second language.

* _____. Así pasamos el día. Illus: Ulises Wensell. (Madrid: Ediciones Altea, 1977. 31p.) Gr. K-2.

A seven-year-old girl and her six-year-old brother charmingly describe one day in their family's life: taking the school bus, painting and eating at school, visiting a bakery shop, visiting grandparents, visiting neighbors, going to the park, going to the doctor, etc. The brief and simple text and the enchanting illustrations will delight young children and also readers who are learning Spanish as a second language.

* _____. Así somos nosotros. Illus: Ulises Wensell. (Madrid: Ediciones Altea, 1977. 31p.) Gr. K-2.

Clara, a seven-year-old girl, and her six-year-old brother, Enrique, tell us about their lives: their visits to the park, their quarrels, their school, their daily activities at home, their baby brother, their parents and their grandparents. The brief and simple text and the enchanting illustrations will delight young children and also readers who are learning Spanish as their second language.

* _____. Así son los abuelos que viven cerca. Illus: Ulises Wensell. (Madrid: Ediciones Altea, 1977. 31p.) Gr. K-2.

A seven-year-old girl and her six-year-old brother delightfully describe their grandparents that live nearby. They tell about Grandma's baking and visit to the beauty shop, and Grandpa's fishing and mechanic garage. They tell about the fun they have together. The brief and simple text and enchanting illustrations will delight young children and also readers who are learning Spanish as a second language.

* _____. Así son los abuelos que viven lejos. Illus: Ulises Wensell. (Madrid: Ediciones Altea, 1977. 31p.) Gr. K-2.

A seven-year-old girl and her six-year-old brother charmingly describe their grandparents that live far away. They have a big two-story home with a big yard. Grandfather is an architect and loves to paint whatever the children ask him to. Grandmother loves music and going to concerts. The children love going to visit them. The brief and simple text and the enchanting illustrations will delight young children and also readers who are learning Spanish as a second language.

* _____. Así son los tíos. Illus: Ulises Wensell. (Madrid: Ediciones Altea, 1977. 31p.) Gr. K-2.

A seven-year-old girl and her six-year-old brother charmingly tell us about their aunt, Isabel, and their uncle, Jorge. They describe various activities they enjoy doing together as well as their aunt and uncle's occupations. The brief and simple text will delight young children and also readers who are learning Spanish as a second language.

* _____. Así son nuestros amigos. Illus: Ulises Wensell. (Madrid: Ediciones Altea, 1977. 32p.) Gr. K-2.

A seven-year-old girl and her six-year-old brother charmingly tell about their friends as well as their parents' friends, their aunt's and uncle's friends, their grandparents' friends and even their dog's friends. The brief and simple text and the enchanting illustrations will delight young children and also older readers who are learning Spanish as a second language.

*   . Así son papá y mamá.   Illus: Ulises Wensell. (Madrid: Ediciones Altea, 1977.   31p.) Gr. K-2.

A seven-year-old girl and her six-year-old brother charmingly tell us about their father and mother.   Both of them work; Papa is an engineer and Mama is a dentist.   Both share life with their children, as well as various housekeeping chores.   They are shown in various work and fun activities.   The brief and simple text will delight young children and also readers who are learning Spanish as a second language.

m Delibes, Miguel.   Mi mundo y el mundo.   (Spain: Editorial Miñón, 1970.   118p.) Gr. 7-12.

The author selected chapters from his works to awaken in adolescents an interest in rural life in Castille; in the life and customs of animals, plants, people and in literature; and in the sad problem of abandoned children.   Most of the selections are depressing fragments of his novels, which I do not believe will appeal to adolescents.   But the last selections, which include the author's impressions of Europe (Naples and Germany), Chile and the United States are delightful reading.   American readers will be amused by a European's view of American cooking habits (weak coffee that can never compare to the real thing, "expresso"); American "fears" of fire, sickness and death; and a most perceptive essay on the beautiful aspects of American education and American children whom the author views as exceptionally talented, honest and spontaneous.

m Díaz-Plaja, Aurora.   Entre juego y juego ... ¡un libro! Illus: María Rius.   (Barcelona: La Galera, 1967. 60p.) Gr. K-2.

Spanish children are shown playing in a city park and when they are tired they enter a children's library. A few traditional library attitudes are described: chil-

79   Spain

dren should wash their hands before handling books,
there should be silence in the library, and no running is
allowed.

m Espinas, Jose María. Todos tenemos hermanos pequeños.
Illus: Sariola. (Barcelona: La Galera, 1968. 10p.)
Gr. K-2.

A story that is meant to teach sympathy and understanding toward abnormal children through the eyes of
other children.

* Ferrán, Jaime. Mañana de parque. Illus: Viví
Escrivá. (Salamanca: Anaya, 1972. 85p.) Gr. K-2.

Gorgeous illustrations of children visiting a zoo; 35
animals are described in humorous detail.

* Fortun, Elena. Celia en el colegio. Illus: Rafael
Munoa. (Madrid: Aguilar, 1973. 225p.) Gr. 3-6.

Celia describes her pranks at a Catholic boarding
school. Humorous adventures show the life of a girl in
Spain and the importance of the Catholic church in a
girl's education.

m Fuertes, Gloria. Aurora, Brígida y Carlos. Illus:
Jan Pienkowski. (Barcelona: Editorial Lumen, 1971.
38p.) Gr. K-2.

Colorful illustrations and attractive presentation,
but unfortunately difficult-to-understand vocabulary detract from this ABC for young children. Each letter
has an accompanying illustration and short verse that
may not be understood by most young children without
extensive explanations of several words and their mean-
ings.

* García Sánchez, José Luis. El Circo 1. Illus: José
Ramón Sánchez. (Spain: Editorial Miñón, 1976. 32p.)
Gr. K-2.

Gorgeous, colorful illustrations and simple, brief
text describe many people that participate in a circus
show: the director, the orchestra, the chorus girls,
strange men and women, magicians, and clowns.

* _____. El Circo 2. Illus: José Ramón Sánchez.
(Spain: Editorial Miñón, 1976. 32p.) Gr. K-2.

Circus animals are portrayed in vivid illustrations:
taming lions, tigers, horses, bears, seals, dogs, elephants, kangaroos and chimpanzees to be ready to per-
form for the circus.

* _____. El Circo 3. Illus: José Ramón Sánchez.
(Spain: Editorial Miñón, 1976. 32p.) Gr. K-2.

In vivid, colorful illustrations and simple, brief
text the reader is exposed to the training and skills of
various circus acrobats.

* García Sánchez, J. L., and M. A. Pacheco. La ciudad
perdida. Illus: Gian Calvi. (Madrid: Ediciones Altea,
1976. 44p.) Gr. 3-5.

A magician is sad to see what human beings do to
their cities: traffic, pollution, noise, destruction of
trees, etc. So, he goes to live in a forest outside the
city. When the people follow him on the weekends, he
notices they also destroy the forest. By using magic,
he makes the city disappear and forces the people to
take better care of it in the future. There are busy
illustrations and a simple text.

* _____ and _____. La escuela encantada. Illus:
Letizia Galli. (Madrid: Ediciones Altea, 1976. 44p.)
Gr. 3-6.

Amusing story with striking illustrations of a fairy
who wanted to go to school. The teacher would not let
the fairy attend school, so the fairy cast a spell: school
was fun, and the children played, ate, painted and did
whatever they wanted to. When fathers came to get their
children, the fathers loved it too. Then mothers came
and also loved school. To get rid of the spell, the
teacher had to allow the fairy in.

* _____ and _____. Los habitantes del planeta
inhabitable. Illus: Dominique Forest. (Madrid:
Ediciones Altea, 1976. 43p.) Gr. 3-5.

Fantasy story with colorful illustrations about a family from another planet that comes to visit the Earth.

81   Spain

They visit the poles but they are too cold; they go to the
bottom of the ocean and find out that marine animals eat
each other up; they go to a desert, but it is too hot.
After visiting other places they don't like they arrive at
a big, crowded city in which they also notice many un-
pleasant things. They return to their planet and state
that the Earth is a good place for vacations but not to
live on.

m _____ and _____. La máquina escarbadora.
Illus: Miguel Calatayud. (Madrid: Ediciones Altea,
1976. 44p.) Gr. 3-6.

Two brothers are constantly engaged in their usual
activities: Doroteo is always inventing things and Teo-
doro is always trying to sell inventions. They dream
that they are going to become famous with Doroteo's
latest invention, but, unfortunately, nobody wants to buy
it. So they continue to dream.... Colorful, modern
illustrations complement the story.

m _____ and _____. Los trabajos del domingo.
Illus: Karin Schubert. (Madrid: Ediciones Altea, 1976.
44p.) Gr. 3-6.

People in a big city are shown performing a variety
of jobs and looking forward to a day of rest. Carpenter,
painter, gardener, office manager, fisherman, cook,
violinist, driver, nurse and mechanic are tired of res-
ting and ready to work again. Busy, colorful illustrations complement the story.

nr Gefaell, María Luisa. Antón Retaco--del ancho mundo.
(Antón Retaco series, VI.) Illus: Pilarín Bayés.
(Madrid: Narcea, 1973. 24p.) Gr. K-2.

Antón goes in search of his godfather and does kind-
nesses along the way. The vocabulary and story are
too difficult for children, and the incidents described
exaggerate the "goodness" of the child.

m _____. Antón Retaco--el bautizo. (Antón Retaco
series, I.) Illus: Pilarín Bayés. (Madrid: Narcea,
1972. 22p.) Gr. 2-5.

Antón and his family travel to many towns performing circus functions. The story emphasizes the impor-

tance of God in Antón's life.   It includes humorous black-and-white cartoons.

nr _____. Antón Retaco--en Villavieja.   (Antón Retaco series, IV.) Illus: Pilarín Bayés.   (Madrid: Narcea, 1973.   24p.)   Gr. K-2.

Mother is expecting a baby so Antón's family decides to settle down in Villavieja.   Antón is shown as a "good" boy helping an old woman clean her house and giving candy to little children.

* _____. Antón Retaco--la función.   (Antón Retaco series, II.) Illus: Pilarín Bayés.   (Madrid: Narcea, 1972.   22p.)   Gr. K-2.

Antón remembers his life with his traveling circus family: his father was the athlete, his mother the acrobat; and there were a goat and a monkey that helped them.   Original black-and-white cartoons complement the simple dialogue.

nr _____. Antón Retaco--los niños tristes.   (Antón Retaco series, V.) Illus: Pilarín Bayés.   (Madrid: Narcea, 1973.   24p.)   Gr. K-2.

Antón is shown making all the town's children happy again.   The children were sad because they didn't understand what caused them to be afraid and Antón decides to try to make them laugh again with his magic tricks.

* _____. Antón Retaco--por los caminos.   (Antón Retaco series, III.) Illus: Pilarín Bayés.   (Madrid: Narcea, 1972.   24p.)   Gr. K-2.

Antón continues describing the characters of his traveling circus family: his father was playful and child-like, his mother was practical and intelligent, his god-father was a dreamer.   He also tells of his own awakening to life.   Graceful black-and-white cartoons illustrate the series.

* Hispano González, Mariano.   Aventura en Australia. Illus: Raymond Cobos.   (Madrid: Plaza y Janés, 1973. 152p.)   Gr. 3-6.

Engaging descriptions of an Australian adventure in

which Pamela Griffin and her adopted children encounter
kangaroos, koalas, crocodiles, and "fierce aborigines."

m _____. Cuentos de siempre. Illus: Angel Badía.
(Barcelona: Afha Internacional, 1972. 77p.) Gr. 3-6.

Three enthralling stories with very well-defined
characters in which there is always an old man with a
very strong personality and a boy. "El capitán Alaska"
describes adventures at sea; "El secreto de Don Marcelo"
condemns war, and "El cazador de leones" relates a
lion-hunting expedition.

nr Ionescu, Angela C. Arriba en el monte. Illus: Adán
Ferrer. (Madrid: Editora Nacional, 1967. 64p.) Gr.
3-6.

Five placid fantasy stories with long descriptions
which may be enjoyed by avid readers who like to read
fanciful stories. It includes, "Arriba en el monte,"
"El secreto del gran elefante," "Buenos días," "Todos
a una," and "La ley del gran jefe."

nr _____. Donde duerme el agua. Illus: Néstor Salas.
(Barcelona: Editorial Labor, 1975. 131p.) Gr. 6-8.

Collection of seven righteous stories that pretend to
instill in young readers love for their own home, hatred
toward war, reverence toward wolves, compassion toward lonely men, and other "good" feelings. Unfortunately, it will only bore most readers.

nr Janer Manila, Javier. El rey Gaspar. Illus: Montserrat Torres. (Barcelona: La Galera, 1976. 96p.)
Gr. 10-12.

The author wrote this book with the intention of
making adolescents "think about a complicated and difficult human problem." King Gaspar illustrates the life
of the immigrant that must leave his home, his family
and his friends in search of a job and a better life.
The main character's pathetic circumstances and depressing thoughts are repeatedly stated: "The world
belongs to those that have money." "Men take advan-
tage of your work." "His life was like a black tunnel
with no escape." "He knew that there wasn't anything
easy, and he must suffer." I doubt that any adolescent

will read this novel and join the author in "thinking" about this serious problem.

* Jiménez-Landi Martínez, Antonio. El campo. Illus: F. Goico Aguirre. (Madrid: Aguilar, 1974. 72p.) Gr. K-2.

Children are exposed to life in the country including farm animals, cultivated farmlands, irrigation, harvest time, arrival of spring, market scenes, picnics, parties, etc. The simple descriptions of the most varied farm activities make this book a delight for young readers despite the spiritless illustrations.

* _____. El circo. Illus: F. Goico Aguirre. (Madrid: Aguilar, 1972. 52p.) Gr. K-2.

Festive illustrations show various circus activities through an extraordinary representation of three puppeteers: circus parade, magicians, rope dancers, acrobats, tigers, bears, leopards and elephants.

m _____. La familia. Illus: F. Goico Aguirre. (Madrid: Aguilar, 1974. 72p.) Gr. K-2.

The members of a family and their work outside the home are explained. Attractive illustrations show mother, father, children, grandparents, uncles, aunts, nieces and nephews and their servants.

* Jover, María Luisa. Yo soy el amarillo. Illus: José Garganté. (Barcelona: La Galera, 1968. 30p.) Gr. K-2.

Simple text and lovely illustrations present the color yellow in things familiar to children: flowers, fruits, animals, sunlight, people of China, etc.

* _____. Yo soy el azul. Illus: José Garganté. (Barcelona: La Galera, 1969. 28p.) Gr. K-2.

Simple text and outstanding illustrations present the color blue, in things familiar to children: the sky, the sea, flowers.

* _____. Yo soy el rojo. Illus: José Garganté. (Barcelona: La Galera, 1968. 31p.) Gr. K-2.

Beautiful illustrations and simple text present the
color red to young children in flowers, fruits, birds,
cars, etc.

m   Kurtz, Carmen. Oscar en Africa.   Illus: Odile Kurz.
(Barcelona: Juventud, 1974.   176p.)   Gr. 3-6.

Fast-moving adventure story in which "bad" white
people are shown abusing the people in Africa.   Oscar
and his friend, Caro, are kidnapped by gangsters in
Africa. After escaping from some dangerous episodes
in which Oscar and Caro discover a gang of drug smug-
glers, Oscar and Caro are lovingly reunited with their
parents.

m   _____. Oscar espeleólogo.   (Barcelona: Lumen,
1973. 204p.) Gr. 3-6.

Engaging adventures of four boys that discover a
magnificent treasure in an underground cave.   Before
rescuing the treasure they have to overcome dangerous
obstacles.   At the end of the story the love and understanding between Oscar and his parents is always emphasized.

*   _____. Oscar espía atómico.   Illus: Carlos María
Alvarez.   (Barcelona: Juventud, 1970.   175p.)   Gr. 3-6.

Imaginative atomic espionage story in which Oscar
discovers a spy who was selling secret formulas.
Through spirited dialogues and vivid adventures, children
are exposed to Spain and its countryside.

m   _____. Oscar y Corazón de Púrpura.   (Barcelona:
Lumen, 1974.   188p.)   Gr. 3-6.

Through daring adventures with gangsters, Oscar
introduces us to the world of scientific fiction.   This is
a fast-moving story of gangsters and deep teenage friendships with entertaining dialogue.

m   _____. Oscar y los hombres rana.   (Barcelona:
Lumen, 1973.   174p.)   Gr. 3-6.

Oscar has dangerous adventures with Arab children
in the Persian Gulf.   After overcoming perilous situations in Chibu-Thani, Oscar, the hero, returns home to
his loving and understanding parents.

nr Lacaci, María Elena.   Tom y Jim.   Illus: Julio Mon-
    tañés.   (Madrid: Doncel, 1966.   113p.)   Gr. 3-6.

    Ten placid stories in which the moral is not even
    thinly disguised.   Pleasing illustrations show Spanish
    children in everyday activities, but the static writing
    style and frail plot line make the book dull and uninter-
    esting.

*   Laiglesia, Juan Antonio de.   Cien nuevos cuentos.   Illus:
    Alda.   (Madrid: Ediciones Recreativas, 1969.   350p.)
    Gr. K-2.

    One hundred enchanting stories for young children
    with engaging illustrations of entertaining themes, such
    as funny pianos, absurd birds, slow buses, and stubborn
    flowers are beautifully presented.

m   Maristany, Manuel.   Rikki-Tikki.   (Madrid: Doncel,
    1969.   130p.)   Gr. 3-6.

    Long adventure story of an African mongoose.   It
    describes the feelings of a mongoose that is finally given
    back its freedom and returned to the African jungle.
    Seven outstanding animal illustrations and lengthy descrip-
    tions make this an appealing story for animal lovers.

nr Mata, Marta.   El país de las cien palabras.   Illus: Ana
    María Riera.   (Barcelona: La Galera, 1973.   16p.)
    Gr. K-2.

    Appealing illustrations but long, difficult-to-under-
    stand descriptions of a country and its people who had a
    vocabulary of only one hundred words.   As the country
    grew, the people realize they needed more words.   A
    poet teaches them the importance of words that describe
    ideas.

m   Mathieu, Renée.   Un fugitivo en el castillo.   Illus:
    Isidre Monés.   (Barcelona: La Galera, 1976.   98p.)
    Gr. 7-12.

    Mystery story that is appropriately set in a small
    Spanish town.   A group of teenage boys and girls, guided
    by their teacher, decide to rebuild a medieval castle
    during their summer holidays.   The group is surprised
    to find out that a stranger is sharing the castle with

them. After a series of strange happenings, the mystery of the "kind" ghost is happily resolved.

m Matute, Ana María. Paulina. Illus: Cesca Jaume. (Barcelona: Lumen, 1969. 153p.) Gr. 3-6.

Original story of a thirteen-year-old girl, Paulina, which describes her concerns: problems with her aunt, relationships with her servants, and compassion toward a blind boy. It describes very well her rural life in Spain and the social differences between rich and poor.

nr _____. El polizón del Ulises. Illus: Cesca Jaume. (Barcelona: Lumen, 1973. 121p.) Gr. 3-6.

Moralistic adventure story in which a boy and a fugitive discuss human injustice and liberty. The boy suffers an accident as he is trying to escape with the fugitive, and the fugitive gives up his freedom to save the boy's life. The story ends with an admonition to children to be "good. "

m Molina, María Isabel. El arco iris. (Madrid: Doncel, 1962. 101p.) Gr. 3-6.

Seven unusual stories with spirited action and various themes: "Los hombres del cielo, " story of a pilot who opposes war, "Los hombres del mar, " men in a whaling ship, "El jinete negro, " warlike story of the Middle Ages, "Los bonzos, " story of some Japanese sculptures, "El guerrero, " American Indians and their relations with white men, "Hombres Negros, " the sale of slaves in Africa, and "Historia escrita en las piedras, " the life of Jesus Christ.

m Morales, Rafael. Dardo, el caballo del bosque. Illus: Ricardo Zamorano. (Madrid: Doncel, 1970. 111p.) Gr. 7-12.

Engaging adventure story of horses, wolves and dogs in which the strong affection between Moncho and his horse, Dardo, is emphasized. The long descriptions may be interesting to horse lovers.

nr Moreno Villa, José. Lo que sabía mi loro. (Madrid: Ediciones Alfaguara, 1977. 60p.) Gr. K-3.

The author collected and illustrated popular Spanish rhymes, riddles and songs as well as his own "golden images. " It includes a few very well-known games, songs, etc. , but the unappealing and confusing presentation (all the text is handwritten with tiny, blurred illustrations) certainly detract from simple enjoyment of the original rhymes.

m   Mussons, Montserrat. Silencio en el bosque. Illus: María Dolz. (Barcelona: La Galera, 1969. 18p.) Gr. K-2.

Gorgeous two-tone illustrations are the background of this story of life in the forest. A lark and a nightingale have a serious disagreement, but in the end harmony prevails, and all is happiness in the forest.

*   Olle, María Angeles. Mi gorrión. Illus: Pilarín Bayés. (Barcelona: La Galera, 1964. 26p.) Gr. K-2.

Simple and sweet story of a girl and her dilemma with a sparrow she found after a snow storm. The girl is shown at home with her mother, grandmother and aunt debating whether to free the bird or put him in a cage.

*   _____. Tula, la tortuga. Illus: Fina Rifá. (Barcelona: La Galera, 1964. 22p.) Gr. K-2.

This is a charming story with beautiful illustrations about Tula, the turtle. A grandmother gives Tula to her grandchildren, who must take care of the turtle. Andresillo is very disappointed when Tula goes to sleep for the winter.

m   Osorio, Marta. El caballito que quería volar. Illus: María Luisa Jover. (Barcelona: La Galera, 1968. 17p.) Gr. K-2.

Original story of the ponies in a merry-go-round and the wishes of one of them to become a bird and fly away. Handsome illustrations show life in a small Spanish town.

m   _____. El gato de los ojos color de oro. Illus: Ma. Antonio Dons. (Madrid: Doncel, 1965. 32p.) Gr. 7-12.

Realistic descriptions and illustrations of gypsies in
Spain who are portrayed through a gypsy family--its
cares and its dances.   It condemns the influence that
money has on human values.   It praises parental and
animal love.

m Pacheco, M. A., and J. L. García Sánchez.   La casa
   que creció.   Illus: M. A. Pacheco.   (Madrid: Ediciones
   Altea, 1976.   44p.)   Gr. 3-6.

A young boy complains because there is nowhere to
play inside of a house.   He cannot play on the streets
because of the cars.   Then he is invited to play with
two sisters who have a large yard.   He decides to water
the sisters' house every day to make it grow.   The house
grows every day until it attracts the police, firemen and
TV people.   So the two sisters and their parents have to
leave their BIG house and move into a new flat with no
yard.   The little boy stops watering the house, which
dries up like a plant.

* _____ and _____ . La granja saltimbanqui. Illus:
   Barbara Druschky. (Madrid: Ediciones Altea, 1976.
   44p.)   Gr. 2-5.

Colorful illustrations and amusing story about a different kind of circus in which all the animals are farm
animals.   Pigs play soccer, cows dance ballet, horses
walk on a tight rope, and sheep jump through a fiery
hoop.   When things start going badly at the circus, the
animals go to live on a farm for a short time.   But they
miss circus life, and when their owner comes back, they
gladly return to their circus.

m _____ and _____ . Limpieza en el bosque. Illus:
   Jesús Camino. (Madrid: Ediciones Altea, 1976.   44p.)
   Gr. 3-5.

Striking colorful illustrations complement a Cinder-
ella in reverse story, in which a princess is searching
for the handsome man who lost his tennis shoe.   In the
meantime, the princess orders clean houses for the
dwarfs, commands exercises be done by the giant, plenty
of rest for the witches, and toothbrushing for the dragon.
Finally, she finds her clean, athletic prince and they get
married.

* _____ and _____ . El reportaje sensacional. Illus:

José Torres. , (Madrid: Ediciones Altea, 1976. 44p.) Gr. 3-6.

A journalist from Jupiter decides to try his luck on the Earth, along with an unsuccessful journalist from the Earth. They write a newspaper story that was printed merely on page 17, they fail at the radio station, they are kept waiting over three hours at the TV station. They finally succeed when they write a bad script for a movie that becomes very popular. The colorful illustrations and simple text will appeal to many readers.

*   _____ and _____ . El viaje de nunca acabar. Illus: Ulises Wensell. (Madrid: Ediciones Altea, 1976. 44p.) Gr. 3-6.

Witty story with attractive illustrations about Augusto and his amazing trip in all kinds of transportation: bus, ship, plane, donkey, camel, train, helicopter, pipeline and car. Finally he decides to mail the cheese to his Aunt Leocadia, as Augusto is going again on another trip.

m   Perera, Hilda. Cuentos para chicos y grandes. Illus: Ana Bermejo. (Spain: Editorial Miñón, 1976. 49p.) Gr. 4-6.

Collection of eight animal stories with a few charming illustrations that gracefully depict animals and/or children. The stories tell about donkeys that are helpful to men, a plebeian puppy who confronts an aristocratic dog, a parrot that misses the trees, the sun and its freedom, etc. Long texts and difficult descriptions make this book recommended only for good Spanish readers.

nr Pérez Lucas, María Dolores. La pajarita sabia. Illus: Ramón Castañer. (Valencia: Marfil, 1969. 32p.) Gr. K-2.

Pleasing illustrations complement this story which moralizes to boys on the need to live peacefully and to avoid reproaching friends.

nr Puncel, María. Operación "pata de oso. " Illus: Ulises Wensell. (Madrid: Doncel, 1971. 120p.) Gr. 3-6.

Educational story that tries to engage the reader through mystery and intrigue. It presents the problem of world starvation and its solution through hydroponic farming. Static writing does not help the story.

m   Rico de Alba, Lolo. Angelita la ballena pequeñita. Illus: José Ramón Sánchez. (Spain: Editorial Miñón, 1975. 46p.) Gr. K-3.

Angelita was a different kind of whale: she was tiny. She tried very hard to grow big like her mama: she ate, she exercised and she rested; but she was still tiny. Finally Angelita decided to find a better place to live. She spent a few unhappy and confusing days in the big city. When she returned home she was delighted to learn that everybody loved her the way she was. This book is very attractively presented with pleasing illustrations, but I am afraid the text may be too long and difficult for young children.

*   _____. Columpio-tobogán-noria gigante. Illus: Miguel Ángel Pacheco. (Spain: Editorial Miñón, 1975. 30p.) Gr. K-2.

Delightful story with adorable illustrations of a giant who wanted to be useful to men. The giant tried helping the trains and the ships go faster, as well as helping the fishermen catch lots of fish, but his actions were not appreciated by men. Not until he noticed children did he realize how he could be useful to them in their games. The simple text will appeal to young children regardless of their knowledge of the Spanish language.

nr _____. Josfa, su mundo y la oscuridad. Illus: Francisco Soro. (Barcelona: La Galera, 1972. 126p.) Gr. 3-6.

Lengthy story that insists on its moral: "People do not love nature. I do not approve of that." And Josfa and his friends discover the reason for people's unhappiness, "They are sad because they have lost contact with nature and therefore they have become selfish." The story has pleasing illustrations but an unengaging writing style.

*   _____. Llorón hijo de dragón. Illus: Miguel Angel Pacheco. (Spain: Editorial Miñón, 1975. 29p.) Gr. K-3.

Amusing story of fierce papa dragon and baby dragon, who wanted to be a boy. Wherever baby dragon cried there appeared many beautiful flowers. So, papa and baby dragon opened a flower shop in the city. In his spare time baby dragon learned to play soccer and eventually made the soccer team. Colorful illustrations beautifully complement the story.

nr _____. El mausito. Illus: José Ramón Sánchez. (Spain: Editorial Miñón, 1975. 29p.) Gr. 1-3.

Mausito asks himself three difficult questions: who am I? How am I? and Where am I? In search of answers he walks through the forest where he meets other animals with whom he must learn to live. The reader is encouraged to know himself, to be happy, and to be able to get along with others. Attractive illustrations but too much deep philosophy for young children.

m Roca, Concepción. El tren que perdió una rueda. Illus: Aurora Altisent. (Barcelona: La Galera, 1972. 16p.) Gr. K-2.

The engine of a small train loses one wheel. The children and animals help the engine run until the old clock serves as the new wheel. Pleasing illustrations and endearing text describe the engine's feelings of gratefulness toward all those who helped him.

m Sadot, Fernando. Cuentos del zodiaco. (Madrid: Doncel, 1971. 112p.) Gr. 3-6.

For young readers interested in astrology, this collection of twelve fantasy stories explains the signs of the zodiac. With pleasing illustrations of each zodiac sign, it describes a lion, a fish, a bull, a girl, etc.

* Sánchez Coquillat, María Marcela. Un castillo en el camino. Illus: Elvira Elías. (Barcelona: Juventud, 1972. 198p.) Gr. 3-6.

Humorous, engaging story that describes the life of two well-to-do Spanish families. The feelings, thoughts and activities in the daily lives of two families are illustrated in black-and-white attractive designs. An adventurous father leads his children into a most exciting holiday at the Costa Brava.

m _____. Han raptado a "Ney." Illus: Elvira Elías.
(Barcelona: Juventud, 1972. 175p.) Gr. 3-6.

Excellent descriptions of the daily life of a Spanish
family which is shown in various activities such as
Spanish Christmas celebrations, professional father at
work, Valencia and orange growing, Spanish food, attractive cities, and beautiful homes. The search for the
family's lost dog provides the setting for the story.

* Sánchez-Silva, José María. Ladis, un gran pequeño.
Illus: José Luis Macías. (Madrid: Marfil, 1971. 39p.)
Gr. 3-6.

Gorgeous illustrations of the Spanish countryside and
its animals provide the background for a sensitive story
of a child who needs fresh, unpolluted air to regain his
health. Ladis' adventures with his friends, the ants,
are a contrast to his poor city bedroom. But poverty,
in this case, is not depressing or hopeless.

* Sola, María Luisa. Ana. Illus: Isidro Monés. (Barcelona: La Galera, 1973. 126p.) Gr. 3-6.

Ana's parents are doctors in Barcelona and have a
maid to do all the housework. Ana's feelings and thoughts
are very well described in a most enjoyable story of a
typical teenager in slacks, long hair, tennis racket,
guitar and records, who goes unwillingly to spend her
summer holidays with her aunt, uncle and cousins in
the country.

* Soler Arce, Carola. El pájaro pinto y otras cosas.
(Madrid: Aguilar, 1954. 112p.) Gr. K-2.

Splendid illustrations and fascinating text, most of
it in verse, describe forty-two themes of interest to
young children, such as animals, "even though I am
little," hats, flowers, and airplanes. It also includes
poems by García Lorca, Amado Nervo and popular
Spanish songs and nursery rhymes.

* Sorribas y Roig, Sebastián. Los astronautas del
"Mochuelo." Illus: Pilarín Bayés. (Barcelona: La
Galera, 1972. 140p.) Gr. 6-10.

Exciting adventures in space with a crew of teenagers which emphasizes respect and understanding toward each other. Girls and boys are shown equally participating in all enterprises in space. Black-and-white illustrations add a humorous touch to the story.

m _____. El zoo de Pitus. Illus: Pilarín Bayés. (Barcelona: La Galera, 1974. 126p.) Gr. 3-6.

The life of a gang of boys in a typical middle-class suburb of Barcelona is very well described through the boys' efforts in setting up a zoo to collect funds for a sick friend. It includes simple illustrations of middle-class people in Barcelona.

m Torrents, Jacint, and Francesc Serrat. El gran dragón. Illus: Carme Solé. (Barcelona: La Galera, 1976. 107p.) Gr. 5-7.

A group of fifty enthusiastic children decide to enliven the town's fiesta by building a secret dragon. They start a well-organized campaign: first collecting old sheets, then various money-producing activities and lastly the actual assembling of the "dragon." The whole town applauds the children's successful dragon and enjoys the wonderful party. Small black-and-white line drawings do not add much interest to the long descriptions. Perhaps only readers with a good knowledge of Spanish might be enthralled with 107 pages of "secret dragon building."

m Valeri, Eulalia. Si yo hiciese un parque. Illus: Antonio Nadal. (Barcelona: La Galera, 1965. 10p.) Gr. K-2.

Modern illustrations show zoo animals as they regain their freedom. A child imagines a park in which animals are not kept behind bars.

nr Vallverdú Aixala, José. Felipe y sus gatos. Illus: Riera Rojas. (Barcelona: La Galera, 1972. 150p.) Gr. 3-6.

This is a lengthy, moralistic story of a man and his cats and his adventures in the mountains: winter storms, a wild boar hunt and wolves are part of the new life of a very well-known sculptor. The moral of the story is that people should help each other.

m _____. Polvorón. Illus: Narmas. (Barcelona: La Galera, 1973. 108p.) Gr. 7-12.

Pleasing illustrations and interesting adventures that show life on a Spanish farm. The story of Polvorón, a dog, and his efforts to regain his freedom and return to his master will be enjoyed by all lovers of dogs.

m _____. Roque, el trapero. (Barcelona: La Galera, 1971. 126p.) Gr. 3-6.

Roque is a boy from the slums who must work to help his poor mother. Black-and-white illustrations show their impoverished home and indigent living conditions. But there is hope for the future: Roque gets an education, Clara, his sick friend, goes to the hospital, and the mother finds a better job.

nr Vázquez Vigo, Carmen. Caramelos de menta. (Madrid: Doncel, 1973. 136p.) Gr. 3-6.

A group of boys finds a lost dog and has several adventures with him. There is an involved incident in which the boys break the covering of a cart which they must pay for. At the end of the story the owner of the dog helps them pay their debt.

* _____. La fuerza de la gacela. (Madrid: Doncel, 1964. 14p.) Gr. 3-6.

Attractive illustrations of animals in the jungle which are shown discussing their fears of a wild tiger. With kindness the beautiful gazelle asks the tiger to behave himself. And the animals live together in peace.

m Vives de Fabregas, Elisa. El globo de papel. Illus: Fina Rifá. (Barcelona: La Galera, 1973. 20p.) Gr. K-2.

Ingenuous story about a paper balloon that is blown away across the skies. It crosses many towns and cities until it is picked up by some children who live by the sea. Graceful illustrations show a happy balloon enjoying the children's gaiety.

* Ydígoras, Carlos María. Landa, el valín. (Madrid: Doncel, 1969. 144p.) Gr. 7-12.

Powerful, moralistic novel that describes the sad life of miners in Spain. It constantly mentions "justice and rotten lungs" and narrates the hardships of a miner family which lost its father in a mine accident.

HISTORICAL FICTION

* Aguirre Bellver, Joaquín. El juglar del Cid. (Madrid: Doncel, 1960. 126p.) Gr. 3-8.

This is a fascinating description of life in Spain during the Middle Ages. It includes the Cid's exile, the Jews, the life of a minstrel and a troubadour, and an outstanding portrayal of the feelings and sufferings of an adolescent boy.

* Blasco Casanovas, Joan. El rescate del pequeño rey. Illus: Lucía Navarro. (Barcelona: La Galera, 1976. 114p.) Gr. 9-12.

The rescue of Jaime I, "The Conqueror," in the spring of 1214 by the heroic efforts of the chivalrous knights, Guillermo de Montcada and Rodrigo del Puy, is full of daring adventure and excitement. It describes the abuses that were committed by the Crusaders and the power of the Pope in Rome. Jaime is portrayed as a very intelligent and perceptive six-year-old boy at the time of his heroic rescue and return to his beloved Barcelona. Readers with a good knowledge of Spanish will enjoy this brief view of life during the Crusades.

* Molina, María Isabel. Balada de un castellano. (Madrid: Doncel, 1970. 92p.) Gr. 7-12.

This is an outstanding historical novel of Spain. It shows Spanish intrigues and life and customs of the Moors and Christians in the year 990. Eight gorgeous illustrations show the people, the cities and the beautiful library in Córdoba.

m _____. Las ruinas de numancia. (Madrid: Doncel, 1969. 90p.) Gr. 7-12.

This is an interesting historical story of life in ancient Rome. It includes descriptions of battles, life and families during a critical time of ancient Rome. Eight splendid illustrations add to the story's appeal.

m   Molina Llorente, María Pilar.   Ut y las estrellas.
    (Madrid: Doncel, 1971.   117p.)   Gr.   5-9.

       Ut is a young man who lived in prehistoric times.
    He does not want to follow his tribe's customs of cruelty
    and violence.   Therefore he is exiled and labeled a cow-
    ard.   This is an engaging novel to discuss cruelty and
    violence.

m   Pérez Avello, Carmen.   Un muchacho sefardí.   Illus:
    Máximo.   (Madrid: Doncel, 1968.   125p.)   Gr.   6-9.

       Unusual narrative which recounts the exile of the
    Jews from Spain in 1492.   It describes the power of the
    Catholic Church and the love of the Jews for the Spanish
    language.   It tries to excuse the attitude of the Spaniards
    toward the Jews by asking, "Which country does not have
    a history of sin and righteousness toward its own chil-
    dren?"

m   Vallverdú, Josep.   Un caballo contra Roma.   Illus:
    Lluis Trepat.   (Barcelona: La Galera, 1976.   118p.)
    Gr.   9-12.

       Through the hardships of a young Iberian slave,
    Aldin, the reader is exposed to the cruelty and power of
    the Roman occupational forces.   Aldin rebels against his
    Roman masters and is constantly punished.   After much
    suffering he recovers his freedom and exchanges the op-
    portunity to live in Rome for a horse.

m   _____ .   Chacales en la ciudad.   Illus: Jordi Bulbena.
    (Barcelona: La Galera, 1977.   123p.)   Gr.   7-10.

       Through the lives of two teenage boys and one girl,
    the reader is exposed to the time when man still lived
    in caves and hunted for food.   As the last remaining
    members of their tribe, they experience moments of
    great difficulty with a ferocious bear and bad weather.
    They are amazed to discover a peaceful group of people
    who lead very different lives.   These strangers are
    farmers who plant food, care for animals, and make
    their own clothes.   After several exciting adventures in
    which the primitive heroes have to prove their friend-
    ship, they all live in peace helping each other in their
    new occupations.

LEGENDS

*   Bravo-Villasante, Carmen, translator. <u>Cuentos populares</u>
<u>de Asia</u>. (Madrid: Doncel, 1976. 170p.) Gr. 4-12.

The Asian cultural center of Unesco sponsored the
collection of these sixteen outstanding legends from India,
Iran, Japan, Korea, Laos, Malaysia, Nepal, Pakistan,
the Philippines, Singapore, Thailand, Viet Nam, Bangla-
desh, and Sri Lanka. The simplicity and spontaneity of
these legends have been beautifully maintained for Spanish readers. This attractive book with beautiful illustrations is a marvelous introduction to ancient Asian cultures.

m   Casona, Alejandro. <u>Flor de leyendas</u>. Illus: F. Goico
Aguirre. (Madrid: Aguilar, 1973. 86p.) Gr. 3-8.

Twelve famous legends from different times and
countries with pleasing illustrations are included in this
attractive collection. Some of the titles are "Guillermo
Tel, " "Las mil y una noches, " "Lohengrin, " "Carta de
Roldán, " and "Hector y Aquiles. "

*   Jiménez-Landi Martínez, Antonio. <u>Leyendas de España</u>.
Illus: Ricardo Zamorano. (Madrid: Aguilar, 1971.
78p.) Gr. 5-10.

This is a splendid collection of nine Spanish legends
of the Middle Ages and the Renaissance period with handsome illustrations. The legends represent diverse Spanish geographic regions, such as Castilla, Asturias,
Galicia, etc.

NON-FICTION

*   Boix, Federico. <u>Papá, ¿cómo nace un niño?</u> (Barcelona: Editorial Nova Terra, 1971. 15p.) Gr. 3-6.

Straightforward approach, with excellent illustrations, to the birth of a child. Simple explanations are
given by the father to a girl and boy upon the arrival of
their new baby brother. Breast-feeding, birth, and affection are effectively explained.

*   García Sánchez, José Luis. <u>El Cine 1</u>. Illus: José

Ramón Sánchez. (Spain: Editorial Miñón, 1976. 32p.)
Gr. 2-4.

Colorful illustrations and simple brief text describe
various types of movies: adventure, mystery, musicals,
science fiction, historical, comical, etc.

*   . El Cine 2. Illus: José Ramón Sánchez.
(Spain: Editorial Miñón, 1976. 32p.) Gr. 2-4.

This book is a brief introduction to the history of
filmmaking; to the important people that make movies--
directors, actors, script writers, electricians, carpen-
ters, photographers, decorators; and to other necessary
items--clothes, animals, etc.

*   . El Cine 3. Illus: José Ramón Sánchez.
(Spain: Editorial Miñón, 1976. 32p.) Gr. 2-4.

Using various film techniques the reader is exposed
to the presentation of "Terror in the Jungle. " Adventure scenes, love scenes and the kind gorilla, Ping-
Pong, are shown in colorful illustrations.

*   . Los Juegos 1. Illus: José Ramón Sánchez.
(Spain: Editorial Miñón, 1976. 32p.) Gr. K-3.

Charming, colorful illustrations and simple, brief
text describe games and toys, where children can play,
with whom can they play, and with what can they play.

*   . Los Juegos 2. Illus: José Ramón Sánchez.
(Spain: Editorial Miñón, 1976. 32p.) Gr. K-4.

Witty, colorful illustrations and brief, simple text
describe various kinds of amusements and games: card
games, chess, ping-pong, fishing, hunting, swimming,
skiing, bowling, gymnastics, motorcycles, pool, dancing,
etc.

*   . Los Juegos 3. Illus: José Ramón Sánchez.
(Spain: Editorial Miñón, 1976. 32p.) Gr. K-4.

Striking, colorful illustrations and simple, brief text
describe various sports and athletic events: basketball,
boxing, horse races, bicycle riding, car races, soccer,
football, Olympic games, etc.

*   . El Teatro 1.   Illus: José Ramón Sánchez.
(Spain: Editorial Miñón, 1976.   32p.)   Gr. 3-6.

This is a marvelous introduction to the theater:
stage settings, actors, amusing, sad and romantic scenes,
etc.   The brief and simple text and humorous illustrations will appeal to many young readers.

*   . El Teatro 2.   Illus: José Ramón Sánchez.
(Spain: Editorial Miñón, 1976.   32p.)   Gr. 3-6.

Splendid illustrations and brief, simple text describe
various types of theatrical presentations: Opera, ballet,
drama, verse, mimicry, tragedy, comedy, puppet show,
etc.   An interesting appendix briefly discusses five
major playwrights and their works.

*   . El Teatro 3.   Illus: José Ramón Sánchez.
(Spain: Editorial Miñón, 1976.   32p.)   Gr. 3-6.

Playful illustrations and brief, simple text describe
the necessary steps to make a theatrical presentation:
writers, producers, directors, designers, decorators,
music, lighting, and public.

m   Gomá, Eulalia.   Diccionario mágico infantil.   Illus:
Jorge Pratmarso.   (Spain: Editorial Vilamala, 1975.
48p.)   Gr. 2-4.

Magic alphabet book that claims to teach new words
and entertain young readers with a magic red filter, but
results in a cluttered, lifeless series of illustrations and
long, complicated definitions.   This book might be useful to readers who would like to increase their vocabulary
in Spanish.

*   Jiménez-Landi Martínez, Antonio.   El libro de los
animales.   Illus: F. Goico Aguirre.   (Spain: Aguilar,
1974.   56p.)   Gr. 3-8.

Pleasing animal illustrations and one-paragraph descriptions tell about many animals' activities, customs,
and lifestyles.   It includes big and small animals from
Europe, America, Asia and Africa.

POETRY

*   Fuertes, Gloria. El hada acaramelada. Illus: Julio
Alvarez. (Madrid: Igreca de Ediciones, 1973. 38p.)
Gr. K-3.

Humorous poems with amusing illustrations that describe children at play, donkeys, hens, flowers, goats,
etc.

m   Madariaga, Salvador de. El sol, la luna y las estrellas.
(Barcelona: Juventud, 1960. 32p.) Gr. K-3.

Madariaga wrote these poems for his granddaughter.
Handsome illustrations about the sun, the moon and the
stars and their friendship with the sky and sea make
this book a pleasure for children.

*   Medina, Arturo, editor. El silbo del aire--antología
lírica infantil. (Barcelona: Vicens-Vives, 1971. Vol.
I, 97p. Vol. II, 125p.) Gr. K-3 & 3-8.

Volume I, for the younger children, contains gorgeous illustrations of simple poems, nursery rhymes,
songs, riddles and games. Some of the authors represented are Rafael Alberti, Gloria Fuertes, Antonio
Machado, Amado Nervo and Lope de Vega. Volume II,
grades 3-8, contains beautiful illustrations of narrative
poems for older children. Some of the authors represented are García Lorca, Juan Ramón Jiménez, Antonio
Machado and Gabriela Mistral.

m   Ribes, Francisco. Poesía de España y América. (Madrid: Santillana, 1968. 123p.) Gr. 7-12.

Good anthology of mostly Spanish poets and a few
Chilean, Mexican, Argentinean, Cuban, Uruguayan,
Nicaraguan and Guatemalan poets. The selctions with
the accompanying illustrations should be interesting to
students whose knowledge of Spanish is such that it will
allow them to enjoy well-known poets in the Spanish
language. Some of the authors represented are: Bécquer,
Asturias, Darío, Góngora, Lope de Vega, Neruda, Nervo,
and Unamuno.

*   Romero, Marina. Alegrías--poemas para niños. Illus:
Sigfrido de Guzmán y Gimeno. (Salamanca: Anaya,
1972. 146p.) Gr. K-2.

Outstanding illustrations and simple poems of things which delight children, such as Peter Pan, Pinocchio, a fox, an ostrich, a macaw, a pigeon, etc.

*   Samaniego, Felix María. Fábulas. (Barcelona: Veron, 1972. 170p.) Gr. 4-12.

Fascinating collection of the famous eighteenth-century fables which should charm all Spanish-speakers. It includes excellent short fables with handsome illustrations.

RELIGIOUS BOOKS

m   Aguirre Bellver, Joaquín. El bordón y la estrella. (Madrid: Doncel, 1961. 121p.) Gr. 5-8.

Story of a pilgrimage to Santiago de Compostela during the Middle Ages in which the religious way of life is emphasized. Powerful characters and exciting adventures maintain the interest of the reader throughout the pilgrimage.

m   Comisión Episcopal de Enseñanza y Catequesis. Con vosotros está, vol. 1. (Madrid: Secretariado Nacional de Catequesis, 1977. 182p.) Gr. 6-10.

This series of four books (see following three entries) prepared by the Church of Spain to guide its young members in their responsibilities to the Catholic Church includes, in the first volume, searching for the Light, Christ is with us, Christ discovers the mystery of God.

m   _____. Con vosotros está, vol. 2. (Madrid: Secretariado Nacional de Catequesis, 1977. 183p.) Gr. 6-10.

The second volume includes Christ discovers the mystery of man: convert! God loves us, even though sinners; We can be new men; Born to faith, hope and love.

m   _____. Con vosotros está, vol. 3. (Madrid: Secretariado Nacional de Catequesis, 1977. 151p.) Gr. 6-10.

The third volume includes: We are a people that

walk, the Church; and Together we shall celebrate a
party without end, the Sacraments.

m _____. Con vosotros está, vol. 4. (Madrid:
Secretariado Nacional de Catequesis, 1977. 128p.) Gr.
6-10.

The fourth volume includes Christ discovers the
mystery of the world; To the new creations; Your works
are prodigious.

m Ferrán, Jaime. Angel en Colombia. (Madrid: Doncel,
1967. 159p.) Gr. 2-5.

Through the eyes of an angel we are introduced to
the people and customs of Colombia. The book emphasizes the importance of talking to the Lord.

m _____. Angel en España. (Madrid: Doncel, 1960.
116p.) Gr. 2-5.

Through the eyes of an angel sent to Spain by the
Lord, the reader visits Cadiz, Jerez, Ronda, Granada
and Barcelona. The angel's purpose is to lighten the
sorrows of all the people he might find on his journey.

m Fuertes, Gloria. El camello cojito (auto de los reyes
magos). Illus: Julio Alvarez. (Madrid: Igreca de
Ediciones, 1973. 38p.) Gr. 1-3.

Beautiful illustrations and simple Christmas poetry
describe strong religious feelings.

m Gefaell, María Luisa. Antón Retaco--el bautizo. See
page 81.

nr Jiménez-Landi Martínez, Antonio. Días sin colegio.
Illus: José Luis Pradera. (Madrid: Aguilar, 1972.
79p.) Gr. 1-6.

This book includes many stories, games and riddles
that children may play or read during the holidays.
Several stories describe the importance of Jesus Christ's
life.

nr Muelas, Federico. Angeles albriciadores. (Madrid:
Doncel, 1971. 137p.) Gr. 2-6.

All the people, animals and things that are described
in these poems explain their happiness because of the
birth of Christ and their wishes to be close to the Lord.

nr _____. Bertolín, una dos ... ¡tres! (Madrid: Doncel, 1962. 99p.) Gr. 3-6.

A sad religious story in which a boy dies after offering his life to the Virgin. This moralistic story describes Spain in the year 1340 and the importance of
religious life.

m Olle, María Angeles. ¿Qué pasa en mi pueblo? Illus:
Fina Rifá. (Barcelona: La Galera, 1968. 10p.) Gr.
K-2.

A Spanish town and its people are shown as they
prepare for Holy Week. They are described decorating
the school, the streets, the town square and the beach.

m Peman, Jose María. Cuentos para grandes y chicos.
Illus: Estadella. (Barcelona: Lumen, 1970. 102p.)
Gr. 3-9.

This is a collection of eight stories about princes
and princesses with humorous characterizations and
comic situations. Two stories emphasize gratefulness
to the Lord through our actions.

nr Salvador, Tomás. Marsuf, el vagabundo del espacio.
(Madrid: Doncel, 1962. 117p.) Gr. 5-10.

This is a religious science fiction story in which
"God, an infinitely superior being, has ordered the cos-
mic magnitude that we are crossing." It emphasizes
love, understanding, forgiveness and the importance of
God.

nr _____. Nuevas aventuras de Marsuf. Illus: Goni.
(Madrid: Doncel, 1971. 127p.) Gr. 5-10.

Marsuf has more adventures in space in which his
love of God, common sense and kindness assure him
success. The story insists on the greatness of God
above all things.

nr Vázquez Vigo, Carmen. Qui qui ri quí. Illus: Pepi

Sánchez. (Madrid: Doncel, 1967. 32p.) Gr. 2-5.

This story centers around the town's church and the town's patron, Saint Francis. The illustrations and text emphasize the significance of religious feelings through an original miracle: a rooster saves the town from burning.

SONGS

* Ribes, Francisco, editor. Canciones de España y América. Illus: Perellón. (Madrid: Santillana, 1965. 84p.) Gr. 1-6.

Fifty-six popular Spanish and Latin American songs and games for children with splendid illustrations have been carefully selected by the editor.

THEATER

m Gasset, Angeles, Títeres con cachiporra. Illus: F. Goico Aguirre. (Madrid: Aguilar, 1969. 84p.) Gr. 3-6.

Five puppet dramatizations with pleasing illustrations which may be performed by children. They are "Los fantasmas," "El gato con capa," "Don Martín el de Aragón," "Patatas" and "Los dos burladores. "

FICTION

nr Capagorry, Juan. Hombres y oficios. Illus: Horacio
Añón. (Uruguay: Ediciones de la Banda Oriental, 1973.
34p.) Gr. 3-8.

Spiritless descriptions of thirteen men of various
occupations, such as blacksmiths, farmer, guitar player,
rural teacher, etc. that claim to recreate the "authentic
atmosphere of Uruguayan towns." The moralizing tone
of each description and the obscure, flat characters result in a tedious book. Lethargic two-tone illustrations
complement the stories.

nr Cunha, Wilda Belura de. La sonrisa del gato o una
manera de pasar el rato. (Uruguay: Fundación Editorial Unión del Magisterio, 1975. 29p.) Gr. 3-6.

Drab book that pretends to amuse children in their
spare time. It includes monotonous "educational" games,
uninspired rhymes and lifeless riddles that will surely
keep children away. The cheap paper and unattractive
presentation underscore a plea that this book not be
shown to children.

nr Da Rosa, Julio C. Buscabichos. (Uruguay: Libros
del Olimar, 1976. 63p.) Gr. 4-8.

The author pretends to write for children because
he remembers his childhood between the ages of five to
ten in which he searched endlessly for "bugs" or living
things, and which then became representative of his
"childhood personality." These are sixteen monotonous
stories about mice, an ostrich, birds, dogs and other
animals that "continue to inhabit the world of the
author's youth. "

nr _____. Gurises y pájaros. Illus: Domingo Ferreira.
(Uruguay: Ediciones de la Banda Oriental, 1973. 47p.)
Gr. 9-adult.

Collection of eleven stories that describe various
types of birds, such as cardinals, owls, woodpeckers,
blackbirds, and others, with human characteristics and
qualities. The author remembers his childhood through
his associations with birds. Bird-lovers might put up
with tedious descriptions of the author's feelings and
thoughts about birds and life.

nr Faedo, Aldo. Recuerdos de la región de las aguas
dulces. (Uruguay: Ediciones de la Banda Oriental,
1974. 35p.) Gr. 7-8.

The author claims to write for young readers through
his reminiscences of his own childhood. In a most affected style, he tediously describes his feelings about
the people and places he knew, his old school, and his
favorite activities that will not interest any reader.

m Gaiero, Elsa Lira. Cancionero del duende verde. Illus:
Humberto Tomeo. (Uruguay: Comunidad del Sur, 1966.
42p.) Gr. 2-5.

Collection of twenty poems about animals, trees,
boats, fruits, and stars that may appeal to children who
have a good understanding of the Spanish language. The
simple illustrations highlight the main ideas in each
poem.

nr García, Serafín J. La vuelta al camino. Illus:
Abelardo Cossio. (Uruguay: Barreiro y Ramos, 1973.
124p.) Gr. 3-6.

Tedious animal stories that include endless descriptions of the mischiefs of a "ñandu" and a fox. Small
black-and-white illustrations and the use of Portuguese
in the narrative do not add to the appeal of these stories.
There is too much text for young readers, and the subject matter won't interest older readers.

nr Ibarbourou, Juana de. El cántaro fresco. (Uruguay:
Editorial Acacia, 1976. 63p.) Gr. 7-12.

Saccharine collection of forty-five poems in prose

in which the author describes her intense feelings towards
nature.   In one-page narratives she expresses her thoughts
about her six-year-old son, the orchard's soul, rainfall,
growing old, the weather, etc.   Cheap paper, insipid,
small, black-and-white illustrations, and uninteresting
writing are not exciting reading material for young readers.

nr   Ipuche, Pedro Leandro.   Chongo.   (Uruguay: Ediciones
Ciudadela, 1968.   45p.)   Gr. 3-6.

Difficult vocabulary and involved situations that pretend to entertain children with the complicated adventures
of a donkey in a "pedagogical" situation and its life at
an educational farm until its death.   The unattractive
presentation, cheap paper, educational intent and color-
less characters will surely discourage any reader from
this book.

nr   Mérola Sóñora, Cecilia.   El niño y el bosque.   (Uruguay:
The Author, 1972.   100p.)   Gr. 3-6.

Through fourteen educational and moralistic lessons,
the author presents a young boy's adventures in the forest.   Readers are taught to work, to save, to be grateful, to be kind, etc. by using examples in the lives of
forest animals.   The unattractive presentation and educational tone of this book will certainly not appeal to any
reader.

nr   Morosoli, Juan José.   Perico.   Illus: Arjax Barnes,
Carlos Pieri.   (Uruguay: Ediciones de la Banda Oriental, 1974.   47p.)   Gr. 2-4.

Uninspired collection of twenty brief stories that
pretend to educate the reader.   The variety of themes
that describe unrelated situations, such as toys, geography, rain, children, etc. does not attract anybody's interest.   And the unattractive presentation, cheap paper,
and drab illustrations do not help this book at all.

m   _____.   Tres niños, dos hombres y un perro.
Illus: Horacio Añón.   (Uruguay: Ediciones
de la Banda Oriental, 1972.   31p.)   Gr. 4-8.

Through the friendship of three boys who meet at
school, the author describes the life of a wealthy family,

a poor farm family, and an orphan black boy. Most of
the descriptions and dialogues of the story are simple
to understand, with the exception of a confusing episode
about God on page 28.

nr Obaldía, José María. 20 mentiras de verdad. Illus:
Horacio Añón. (Uruguay: Ediciones de la Banda
Oriental, 1973. 46p.) Gr. 4-8.

Twenty spiritless stories that deaden the interest of
any reader. Unattractive format, absurd situations, and
dull writing make these stories about animals, people
and toys an extreme waste of time. The monotonous
two-tone illustrations don't help too much either.

nr Pesce, Elena. El canguro bizco. Illus: Jaime Parés.
(Uruguay: Ediciones de la Banda Oriental, 1970. 38p.)
Gr. 3-6.

It is hard to believe that this book won a children's
literature award in Uruguay in 1969. The confusing illustrations and perplexing descriptions about Little
Falcon's wishes of having his own "Protective Spirit, "
make this fantasy story difficult to read and impossible
to enjoy. A cross-eyed kangaroo, Indian priests, Old
Turtle and sacred Gods from Tenochtitlán are some of
the flat characters that dominate this absurd, slow-
moving story.

*   Quiroga, Horacio. Los cuentos de mis hijos. Illus:
Yenia Dumnova. (Uruguay: Arca Editorial, 1970. 80p.)
Gr. 6-10.

Ten entertaining animal stories written by the well-
known Uruguayan author, Horacio Quiroga, for his children. The stories show Quiroga's deep interest in
hunting as well as his concern for and knowledge of animals. Simple black-and-white illustrations add an
amusing humor to the stories.

m   _____. Las medias de los flamencos. (Uruguay:
Consejo Nacional de Enseñanza Primaria, 1972. 23p.)
Gr. 3-6.

Fast-moving text and two-tone line illustrations tell
the story of the flamingos that used to have white feet
but now have red feet. Young readers might enjoy being

exposed to this well-known Uruguayan author through this clever animal story, but some of the vocabulary words will have to be explained to them.

HISTORY

m Mendez Vives, Enrique. La gente y las cosas en el Uruguay de 1830. (Uruguay: Ediciones Tauro, 1969. 93p.) Gr. 6-10.

History of Uruguay that describes various aspects of life in 1830. Even though the cheap paper and unattractive presentation might make this book unappealing to many readers, it does have valuable historical glimpses and insights that could be useful to those readers interested in Colonial times in Uruguay. Such aspects as exports and imports, family life, the slave trade, transportation and education are among those covered. It is written in a matter-of-fact way, with news, announcements and public commentaries of the times.

POETRY

nr Fernandez, Julio. Girasol de la mañana. Illus: José Gómez. (Uruguay: Ediciones de la Banda Oriental, 1974. 44p.) Gr. 3-10.

Collection of twenty-five saccharine poems about dreams, ants, spring, birds, rest, Sunday, etc. , that were written "to develop and elevate the sensibility of the child. " Neither the sophisticated vocabulary, nor the vague ideas expressed in these poems will interest young readers. The decorative two-tone illustrations are simpler, therefore, "prettier. "

nr Neira, Luis, and José María Obaldía. Versos y canciones en la escuela. Illus: Edda Ferreira. (Uruguay: Ediciones de la Banda Oriental, 1973. 47p.) Gr. 7-10.

Collection of thirty-five obtuse poems for students selected by the authors because "they work on the sensibility of the child as well as transmit knowledge. " The themes include topics that are "intimately related to children's interests," as stated in the authors' prologue. The result is a collection of uninspired, pretentious poems about the seasons, dreams, toys, nature, and America.

VENEZUELA

BIOGRAPHY

nr Ayala, Key S. Vida ejemplar de Simón Bolívar.
(Venezuela: Ediciones Edime, 1976. 196p.) Gr. 9-12.

Pretentious biography of Bolívar, the South American leader of the independence movement in the nineteenth century, written by the author to teach young adults to love and to admire Bolívar. In the most didactic, sermonizing style the author used Bolívar's life to serve as an example of a patriotic hero for all young readers. Unfortunately the author preached too much and didn't even offer the reader insights into Simón Bolívar's life.

m Salcedo-Bastardo, J. L. Un hombre diáfono. (Venezuela: Cultural Venezolana, S. A. , 1977. 166p.) Gr. 7-10.

This biography of Simón Bolívar was intended by the author to show the South American liberator as a hardworking, courageous and generous patriot. It describes important facts of the hero's life in simple-to-understand language. Unfortunately the author preaches to adolescents too insistently about imitating Bolívar's superb qualities and virtues. At the end of every chapter there is a patriotic or moral lesson that the author believes adolescents should learn and adapt into their own lives.

FICTION

* Almoina de Carrera, Pilar. El camino de Tío Conejo.
(Venezuela: Ministerio de Educación, 1970. 75p.) Gr. 2-5.

Delightful collection of twenty Venezuelan folktales

111

that amuse the readers with the adventures of Uncle Rabbit and Uncle Tiger.   Simple text and colorful illustrations show little Uncle Rabbit constantly outsmarting powerful Uncle Tiger.   The brevity of these tales (mostly two pages long) and the entertaining situations described will certainly be enjoyed by many young readers and/or listeners.

nr   Bracho, Evaristo A.   Manchita.   Illus: Agustín Hidalgo Sajo.   (Venezuela: Ministerio de Educación, 1974.   39p.) Gr. 3-6.

Tedious collection of ten stories for children about a dog that went to school, children's questions, America, a teacher's comments, friendship, etc.   Long descriptions and unappealing sermons contrast with the attractive illustrations.   Children will be bored by these stories.

nr   Caldera, Alicia Pietri de, editor.   Más páginas para imaginar.   (Venezuela: Ediciones Fundación Festival del Niño, 1972.   173p.)   Gr. 3-6.

Dull collection of thirty stories and poems inappropriately selected by the editor to provide to children "gentle, kind and truly childlike literature. "   Unappealing illustrations and endless educational stories about being prompt to school, respecting your flag, valuing your work, etc. might win a few Venezuelan children literature prizes to their authors, but will certainly not amuse young readers.

nr   _____.   Siempre páginas para imaginar.   (Venezuela: Ediciones Fundación Festival del Niño, 1973.   172p.) Gr. 3-6.

Uninteresting collection of thirty-two stories, poems and songs written to provide to children a message of "kindness, happiness, and hope. "   Stilted illustrations and long, dull descriptions insist on "good" behavior appropriate to flower vases, animals, the wind, rainbows, and the like.   Other stories pretend to educate children about the growth of corn, good manners among neighbors, etc.   This book results in too many wasted pages.

nr   Egui, Luis Eduardo.   El pequeño mundo de Juan Luis. (Venezuela: Editorial Mediterráneo, 1971.   199p.)   Gr. 7-12.

Long collection of episodes in the life of Juan Luis,
a Venezuelan boy. His father is from Italy and his
mother is a Venezuelan Indian. It is repetitive in its
presentation of ideas and writing style. Too many of
the episodes are dull with long descriptions and uninteresting situations about school and university life, fruit,
literature, death, grammar, languages, and so on.
There is no continuity to hold the reader's attention in
the various sections. Of interest may be the section on
Rómulo Gallegos, the Venezuelan author (pages 108-114).

m   Padrino, Luis. Relato de un niño indígena. (Venezuela:
Editorial Latorre, 1938. 165p.) Gr. 3-6.

Short historical anecdotes as seen through the eyes
of young Venezuelan Indian children written in simple,
easy-to-understand language. Unfortunately the emphasis
is strongly educational and moralistic and it indicts Indian men as lazy and as heavy drinkers. It does offer interesting insights about Venezuelan pre-Columbian life
such as that Indian men had to buy their wives before
marriage, and they did not have a written language or
a written numerical system. The second part includes
brief chapters during the Spanish Conquest and Colonial
periods of Venezuela.

*   Rivero Oramas, Rafael. El mundo de Tío Conejo.
(Venezuela: Ministerio de Educatión, 1973. 173p.)
Gr. 2-5.

Delightful collection of eighteen popular Venezuelan
stories that describe the constant misunderstandings between Uncle Rabbit and Uncle Tiger. In an easy-to-read
manner the author narrates the cleverness of Uncle Rabbit in outwitting Uncle Tiger. Young readers will delight in reading these animal stories full of excitement
and adventure, even though some of the illustrations are
too crowded and obscure.

m   Tinajero, Martín. Navidad del niño venezolano. (Venezuela: Editorial Avila Gráfica, 1950. 29p.) Gr. 3-6.

Venezuelan Christmas celebrations are interestingly
portrayed with attractive two-color illustrations. It describes "Misas de aguinaldo, " popular foods, and their
preparations, popular songs and customs, and unique
Venezuelan Christmas festivities. Unfortunately the qual-

ity of the paper does not make it too appealing to most readers.

nr   Van Egmond, Robert. Burbujas. (Venezuela: Ministerio de Educación, 1974. 95p.) Gr. 2-6.

Attractive striking illustrations in color illustrate a book that was written "to liberate the economic, social, cultural and spiritual Hispanic American being, and to resist the cultural dependency." The complex vocabulary expresses vague descriptions of ideas and feelings, such as, "El dolor llega a su alma, pero dolor mil veces prefiere si con ello ve cubrirse de oro sus negras ramas" (p. 24). The only stories that may appeal to children are "El Nahual" (pp. 31-35), the Guatemalan legend of their beloved Quetzal, and "Nanduti" (p. 65-70), a Paraguayan legend of the beautiful mantillas.

MAGAZINE

*   Tricolor. (Venezuela: Ministerio de Educación, monthly magazine.) Gr. 1-8.

Attractive monthly magazine for children that includes articles and stories on children's literature and art, natural and social sciences, environmental protection, games, and a charming poster for young children on various recreational themes. The diversity of its content and appealing format might attract many young readers. Free to schools and libraries.

NON-FICTION

nr   Noguera, Nicolas H., and Raquel Citty Pithol. El calendario de mis recuerdos. (Venezuela: Distribuidora Nimar, 1972. 109p.) Gr. 3-6.

Monotonous collection of fifty-two readings that follows the Venezuelan school calendar with all its important patriotic, social and religious holidays. Unfortunately the small, unappealing, black-and-white illustrations and the brief, didactic descriptions of each holiday might only be used for teachers as a factual reminder of Venezuelan holidays, but children need not be exposed to such dull reading.

* Qüenza, Samuel Eduardo. Hablemos de nuestra América.
(Venezuela: Ministerio de Educación, 1974. 89p.) Gr.
7-12.

   Written for students to learn more about Latin
America, this book is divided into the following sections:
I--Selected paragraphs of Spanish-speaking authors, such
as Jose Martí, Miguel Cervantes Saavedra, Pablo Neruda,
Gabriel García Márquez, etc. ; II--Photographs and basic
facts of Latin American cities, such as Mexico City,
Buenos Aires, Caracas, Guatemala; III--Need for economic development, emphasizing that "Tenemos necesidad
de conquistar nuestra independencia económica" (p. 34),
and other interesting aspects of South Latin America,
such as, geography, customs, heroes, etc. Very good
publication that highlights in simple concise language
important facts of Latin America.

POETRY

nr Bosch, Velia. Arrunango. (Venezuela: Instituto
Nacional de Cultura y Bellas Artes, 1968. 47p.) Gr.
3-6.

   Spiritless collection of eighteen poems for children
about animals, trips, days of the week, and dreams,
that bore readers with their sophisticated style and pretentious messages.

nr Carrillo, Morita. ¡Tilingo! (Venezuela: Oficina Cen-
tral de Información, 1966. 24p.) Gr. 3-6.

   Uninspired religious poems that narrate the birth of
Jesus, Christmas Day in Venezuela, and the Virgin
Mary's love, with complicated vocabulary and long,
tiring descriptions. Bold children's illustrations are
the only appealing feature.

nr _____ . Torres de celofán. Illus: Halina Mazepa
de Koval. (Venezuela: Instituto de Cultura y Bellas
Artes, 1968. 62p.) Gr. 3-6.

   Lifeless poems for children about animals, the wind,
the sea, the sun, etc. with complex descriptions and
moralistic situations, which bore any child who attempts
to enjoy them. Only the seven simple animal illustrations will attract any reader.

nr Machado Fernández, Arturo. Mentiras de algodón.
(Venezuela: Secretaría de Educación Edo. Carabobo,
1976. 43p.) Gr. 5-9.

   Pretentious collection of twenty-eight poems for
children written by the author for the purpose of "offering
a clean service to the community." The author pretends
to amuse children with his religious thoughts about God's
good actions, the differences in color among fellow hu-
mans, the Virgin's constant protection of children's
sleep, etc. Four line illustrations decorate this book
that no child will enjoy.

m   Mendoza Sagarzazu, Beatriz. Tarea de vacaciones.
Illus: Lola Altamira. (Venezuela: Artegrafía, 1977.
34p.) Gr. 3-6.

   Attractive illustrations complement these poems
about a paper boat, rain, arts, a kite, a scarecrow,
grasshoppers, vacation activities, etc. Unfortunately,
the vocabulary used may be too difficult for most children.

nr Muñoz Tebar M., Consuelo. Pequeño mundo infantil.
(Venezuela: no publisher or date given, 30p.) Gr. 2-4.

   Uninspired collection of forty-one poems describing
the author's feelings about God, children's guardian
angels, the importance of washing one's hands, mothers'
love, respect to Venezuela's flag, etc. Seven stilted
illustrations do not add much to this basically boring,
didactic collection of poems.

nr Osses, Ester María. Crece y camina. (Venezuela:
Editorial Universitaria de la Universidad del Zulia, 1971.
103p.) Gr. 3-8.

   Sophisticated collection of forty-two poems that, even
though some describe the author's memories as a child,
will not be of interest to children. The poems tell about
the author's happiness in talking to her mother on the
telephone, about her friendship with grateful plants,
about liberating imprisoned birds and fish, etc. Only a
few of the well-known riddles included will appeal to
children.

nr Paz Castillo, Fernando. La huerta de Doñana. (Venezuela: Ediciones Tricolor, 1969. 83p.) Gr. 6-12.

Obscure love poem written in the 1920's about an
older woman and the unfortunate innocent love affair of
her youth. Perhaps the author had children in his mind
when he included children's games and special educational
messages for young readers, such as "Cuando el cuerpo
está sucio el alma no puede estar limpia" (when the body
is dirty, the soul cannot be clean). Its long, vague descriptions will certainly not interest any reader.

nr   Rodríguez, Ernesto Luis. Arriba capitán. Illus: María
     Valencia. (Venezuela: Instituto Nacional de Cultura y
     Bellas Artes, 1968. 63p.) Gr. 3-6.

Tedious poems which moralize to children about
school, the value of education, mothers' love, etc. They
are unappealing because of their presumptuous tone and
affected vocabulary.

nr   Rosas Marcano, Jesus. Manso vidrio del aire. (Vene-
     zuela: Instituto Nacional de Cultura y Bellas Artes,
     1968. 79p.) Gr. 3-10.

Tiresome poems about animals, geography, city life,
oil, newspapers, Christmas, etc. that cannot possibly
interest young readers. Its complicated vocabulary and
ostentatious admonitions are unappealing and dull.

nr   Rovero de Perez Guevara, Flor. Bebedero de rocío.
     (Venezuela: Ministerio de Educación, 1975. 76p.) Gr.
     3-6.

Dull collection of twenty-five poems that the author
wrote "to clean the children's imaginations of bad influences and to suggest to them tender and sweet thoughts."
The result is an affected collection of the author's memories as a child, her feelings about showing tenderness
to all children, her love towards her grandmother, etc.
Five stilted animal illustrations complement this uninspired collection.

nr   Rugeles, Manuel F. Canta Pirulero. Illus: Serny.
     (Venezuela: Jaime Villegas, 1954. 73p.) Gr. 3-6.

Collection of monotonous and uninspired poems for
children which describe complex thoughts and awkward

situations, even though the themes are common to all
children, such as, flowers, animals and nature. Example: "Muda, la tierra levanta los árboles del camino, y
el cielo dice a los pajaros:--¡Haced música en los nidos!"
(p. 33). The following two games may appeal to some
children: "Las tres perseguidas" (p. 64-65) and "Los
artesanos" (p. 70-71).

m   Subero, Efraín, editor. Poesía infantil venezolana.
    (Venezuela: Ediciones Centauro, 1977. 285p.) Gr.
    1-10.

    Anthology of Venezuelan poems carefully selected by
the editor "to encourage in children an interest in good
literature and the habit of reading." The editor intended
this anthology to be used by teachers in schools; therefore, he divided the poems into grade levels (K-1, 2-3,
4-5). The last 90 pages provide an interesting sample
of Venezuelan folklore, which I believe is the best part
of the anthology. It includes popular romances, riddles,
children's songs, tongue twisters, Indian songs, etc.,
that maintain the freshness and spontaneity of the Spanish language without the didacticism or moralism underscored in many of the modern poems for children in the
first part of the anthology.

                        THEATER

nr Subero, Efraín. Teatro Escolar. (Venezuela: Minis-
    terio de Educación, 1970. 438p.) Gr. 3-9.

    Wearisome collection of forty-four educational and
moralistic plays written by thirteen Venezuelan authors
published in the magazine Tricolor in the last twenty
years. The plays exalt moral values, national pride,
well-known heroes, the importance of education, and
love of nature with a total disregard of the recreational
or entertainment needs of young readers.

Appendix I

BOOK DEALERS IN SPANISH-SPEAKING COUNTRIES

ARGENTINA

Sr. Fernando García Cambeiro
Avenida de Mayo 560
Buenos Aires, Argentina

CHILE

Fontana, Servicio Bibliográfico
Ramón Perez G.
Casilla 5602
Santiago 2, Chile

COLOMBIA

Libros de Colombia
Apartado Aéreo 12053
Calle 22-F No. 42 C-37
Bogotá, Colombia

COSTA RICA

Librería Lehmann, S. A.
Apdo. 10011
San José, Costa Rica

CUBA

Librería las Américas
2015 Boul. St. Laurent
Montreal, Quebec
Canada

ECUADOR

St. Jorge Eduardo Jiménez Jiménez
General Pintag 511 y Jauja
Ciudadela Hermano
Miguel, La Magdalena
Quito, Ecuador

MEXICO

Sra. Pilar S. de Gómez   Librería Porrúa Hnos.
P I G O M   Av. Rep. Argentina
Parque España 13-A   y Justo Sierra
México 11, D. F.   México 1, D. F.

PERU

Librería Juan Mejía Baca
Jirón Azángaro 722
Lima, Perú

PUERTO RICO

Thekes, Inc.
Plaza las Américas
Hato Rey, Puerto Rico   00918

SPAIN

Libros Talentum
Núñez de Balboa, 53
Madrid 1, España

URUGUAY

Barreiro y Ramos, S. A.
25 de Mayo 604
Casilla de Correo 15
Montevideo, Uruguay

VENEZUELA

Soberbia C. A.
Avenida La Industria No. 4
Puente Anauco
Caracas 101, Venezuela

Appendix II

UNITED STATES BOOK DEALERS
(That Specialize in Books in Spanish)

Adler's Foreign Books
162 Fifth Avenue
New York, NY 10010

Hector H. Bravo
1204 West 7th Street
Los Angeles, CA 90017

Iaconi
300 Pennsylvania Avenue
San Francisco, CA 94107

Larousse and Co.
572 Fifth Avenue
New York, NY 10036

Quality Books, Inc.
400 Anthony Trail
Northbrook, IL 60062

Rizzoli International
712 Fifth Avenue
New York, NY 10019

Spanish Book Corporation of America
115 Fifth Avenue
New York, NY 10003

Spanish Book Store
2326 Westwood Blvd.
Los Angeles, CA 90064

AUTHOR INDEX

123

Author Index 126

TITLE INDEX

SUBJECT INDEX

139

MYTHS
  Barrionuevo, A.: El Muki y otros personajes fabulosos
  59
NATURE
  Canela Garayoa, M.: ¿De quién es el bosque? 73
  Delibes, M.: Mi mundo y el mundo 78
  Estrada, S.: Un día en la vida de Juan Trébol 3
  Ibarbourou, J.: El cántaro fresco 107
  Izquierdo Ríos, F.: El colibrí con cola de pavo real 56
  Prado, P.: Alsino 28
  Rico de Alba, L.: Josfa, su mundo y la oscuridad 91
  Sánchez-Silva, J. M.: Ladis, un gran pequeño 93
  Serrano Martínez, C.: El cazador y sus perros 50
OCCUPATIONS
  Capagorry, J.: Hombres y oficios 106
OCEAN
  Capdevila, J.: Teo en barco 73
ORPHANS
  Martin, S.: Aventuras de dos muchachos que buscaban
  un papá 9
OTAVALO INDIANS
  Buitrón, A.: Taita Imbabura-vida indígena en los Andes
  44
PARENTS
  D'Atri, A.: Así son papá y mamá 78
PICTURE BOOK
  Nieves Falcón, L.: Poemas y colores 63
PLAY
  Cunha, W. B. de: La sonrisa del gato o una manera de
  pasar el rato 106
POETRY
  Aguirre, M.: Juegos y otros poemas 42
  Bosch, V.: Arrunango 115
  Carrera, C.: Nueva poesía infantil 45
  Carrillo, M.: ¡Tilingo! 115
  Carrillo, M.: Torres de celofán 115
  Cifra, A.: Las poesías de Mari Pepa 17
  Fernández, J.: Girasol de la mañana 110
  Fuertes, F.: El hada acaramelada 101
  Gaiero, E. L.: Cancionero del duende verde 107
  Galimerti de Guacci, H.: Canto al amanecer 18
  Hernández, Jose: Martín Fierro 18
  Jara Azócar, O.: Operación alegría 30
  Machado Fernández, A.: Mentiras de algodón 116
  Madariaga, S. de: El sol, la luna y las estrellas 101
  Medina, A.: El silbo del aire--antología lírica infantil
  101

149   Subject Index

Mendoza Sagarzazu, B.: Tarea de Vacaciones 116
Muñoz Tebar M., C.: Pequeño mundo infantil 116
Neira, L., y J. M. Obaldía: Versos y canciones en la escuela 110
Núñez, A. R.: Escamas del Caribe 42
Olave, M. del P.: Poesía menuda 60
Osorio, F.: Lección de poesía 33
Osses, E. M.: Crece y camina 116
Paz Castillo, F.: La huerta de Doñana 116
Ribes, F.: Poesía de España y América 101
Ríos, L.: Algodón de azúcar 37
Rodríguez, E.: Luis Arriba capitán 117
Romero, M.: Alegrías--poemas para niños 101
Romero, M.: Los mejores versos para niños 30
Rosas Marcano, J.: Manso vidrio del aire 117
Rovero de Pérez, G.: Flor Bebedero de rocío 117
Rugeles, M. F.: Canta pirulero 117
Sáenz, C. L.: El viento y Daniel 37
Subero, E.: Poesía infantil venezolana 118
Vettier, A., y N. Grisolía: Alfombra mágica 18
Walsh, M. E.: Tutú marambá 18
Walsh, M. E.: Versos tradicionales para los cebollitas 19

POLITICAL NOVEL
Fallas, C. L.: Mamita Yunai 35
POLLUTION
Cuadrench, A.: Erase una vez un pueblo 75
POVERTY
Vallverdú Aixala, J.: Roque, el trapero 95
PUERTO RICO
Ribes Tobar, F.: Puerto Rico en mi corazón 66
RED
Jover, M. L.: Yo soy el rojo 84
RELATIONSHIPS
García Monge, J.: El moto 36
RELIGIOUS STORIES
Aguirre Bellver, J.: El bordón y la estrella 102
Caballero Calderón, E.: La historia en cuentos 34
Ferrán, J.: Angel en Colombia 103
Ferrán, J.: Angel en España 103
Fuertes, F.: El camello cojito. (auto de los reyes magos) 103
García Mejía, H.: Cuento para soñar 34
Gefaell, M. L.: Antón Retaco, el bautizo 81
Jiménez-Landi Martínez, A.: Días sin colegio 103
Muelas, F.: Angeles albriciadores 103
Muelas, F.: Bertolín, una dos ... ¡tres! 104